The Name Is the Game
How to Name a Company or Product

The Name Is the Game

How to Name a Company or Product

By
Henri Charmasson

Dow Jones-Irwin
Homewood, Illinois 60430

This publication is designed to provide accurate and
authoritative information in regard to the subject matter
covered. It is sold with the understanding that the
publisher is not engaged in rendering legal, accounting, or
other professional service. If legal advice or other expert
assistance is required, the services of a competent
professional person should be sought.

*From a Declaration of Principles jointly adopted by a Committee
of the American Bar Association and a Committee of Publishers.*

Acquisitions editor: Susan Glinert Stevens Ph.D.
Production manager: Charles J. Hess
Designer: Renée Klyczek Nordstrom
Compositor: Carlisle Communications Limited
Typeface: 11/13 Century Schoolbook
Printer: R. R. Donnelley & Sons Company

ISBN 1-55623-069-9

Library of Congress Catalog Card No. 87–71545

Printed in the United States of America

1 2 3 4 5 6 7 8 9 0 DO 5 4 3 2 1 0 9 8

CONTENTS

Preface   ix

Dedication and Acknowledgments   xiii

PART 1 THE PRINCIPLES   1

CHAPTER 1 Preliminaries   3

Good Commercial Names Are Not Found. A Name Is
a Promise. Definitions. The Mechanics of
Commercial Names. Borrowing or Coining the
Name. A Rose Named Slime Would Not Sell Well.
Watch Your Language. An Art and a Science.

CHAPTER 2 The Role of Commercial Names   12

Promotion. Protection. Profit.

CHAPTER 3 Names to Avoid   20

Pride of the Peacock. Definitions. Thou Shalt Not
Steal. Alphabet Soup. Scarecrows, Skeletons, and
Scatology.

CHAPTER 4 Anatomy of a Good Name   32

Greyhound. Jellibeans. Nyquil. Kodak. Hang Ten.

CHAPTER 5 Legal Factors   39

Degrees of Strength. Enforceability: *Scope of
Monopoly, Summary Proceedings*. High Wire Act.

PART 2 THE METHOD 47

CHAPTER 6 Outline 49

Overview. Start with a Clean Slate. Dealing with the Ad-man. Dealing with the B.O.D.

CHAPTER 7 Gathering the Facts 56

Defining the market: *Territory, Field of Use, The Customer.* Defining the Product or Services. Product Life. Examples.

CHAPTER 8 The Message 66

Sorting the Promotional Factors. The Commercial. Advertising Fundamentals. The Synthesis.

CHAPTER 9 Nuts and Bolts 74

Borrowing the Name. Symbolism. Metonymy. Allusion or Evocative Reference. Onomatopes. Rhythm and Poetry. Humor. Application.

CHAPTER 10 Coining the Name 83

Composition. Fusion. Tacking and Clipping. Mimicking Monikers. Analogy. Semantation. Ideophones. Multimedia Names.

CHAPTER 11 Construction Material 93

Quarry Stones. Used Bricks. Family of Names. Be Original.

CHAPTER 12   Graphy, Design, and Logo   **101**

Spelling. Typesetting. Design and Logo. Character
Names. Recapitulation. Hold the Verdict.

CHAPTER 13   The Name Availability Search   **111**

The Issues. Infringement. Enforceability.
Registrability. Intrinsic Value.

CHAPTER 14   Picking the Winner   **121**

Preliminary Screening. Legal Strength. Marketing
Factors. Grading Exercise. Delivery.

CHAPTER 15   Name Acquisition and Registration   **134**

Use in Commerce. Avoiding Loss of Ownership.
Markings and Statutory Notices. Registration.

Conclusion   **143**

Legal References   **145**

Glossary of Technical Terms   **153**

Bibliography   **157**

Index   **159**

PREFACE

Have you ever gone through the maddening chore of devising a corporate identifier for your new firm or a brand name for a new product? Did you discover that the eye-popping name you settled upon after many frustrating hours of research had already been taken or that only a few yes-men in your organization appeared to like it? Perhaps your questing zeal for an inspiring moniker has flagged to the point where you are about to settle for the first available name you can find? By now, you might even have come to envy those entrepreneurs who took refuge in N.B.I. (Nothing But Initials) and TOLFAN (Tired Of Looking For A Name).

If this is any consolation, you are in good company. In his book *Ogilvy on Advertising*, marketing mogul David Ogilvy admits that finding any usable name that has not already been registered by another company is infernally difficult. "I have suggested names for dozens of new products," says he, "but have not yet had one accepted."

How does one find commercial names on a par with KODAK, GREYHOUND, APPLE, FORMICA, TEFLON, SUNKIST, or RAINBIRD? In the words of poet Charles Swinburne: "Bright names that men remember!"

Most of what has been written on this subject is hidden away beyond the reach of ordinary business people in esoteric treatises on trademark law. The articles appearing sporadically in various professional publications usually limit themselves to anecdotal accounts of the selection of specific corporate or brand names.

This paucity of information is due neither to lack of interest in the subject nor to the absence of a demand for new names. Around six hundred thousand businesses are launched every year in the United States, and every one of these requires a new identifier. About the same number of new products are introduced and need to be branded. Changes in the names of existing products and companies increase the demand still further. How is this need for new monikers satisfied? Very poorly indeed. The U.S. Patent and Trademark Office adds about seventy-five thousand new entries per year to the near one million marks already recorded in its registers. This leaves in circulation, of each year's crop, several thousand brand names of questionable legitimacy or commercial value. The large number of duplications and imitations feed a steady stream of infringement litigations into the judicial system, to the delight of trial lawyers and the despair of the large and small entrepreneurs engulfed in this quagmire.

A survey of contemporary commercial naming practices reveals many empirical approaches marred by a total lack of objectivity. The most popular method involves the compilation of a long list of plausible words and then the selection from that list of a name that appears to be best suited for the job. Some have expedited the process by programming a computer to spit out random combinations and permutations of letters and syllables until they hit upon a good prospect. A consultant once submitted to the management of Consolidated Foods six hundred variations on that name in an attempt to resolve a company identity crisis. An executive panel scanned the list but could not agree on any of the proposed names. The result is not surprising. The name candidates were generated by a machine without rhyme or reason. It is questionable whether the executives themselves knew what they should have been looking for in the first place. Consolidated Foods resolved the problem by adopting one of its most successful brand names— SARA LEE—as a new corporate identifier, wisely dodging the thorny issue of creating a new name.

Other companies prefer to organize a public or in-house name selection contest. This makes as much sense as practicing medicine by popular vote. The result can be most unpredictable and of dubious quality at best. A contest requires a winner, whether or not the proposed name is acceptable. The promoter may be saddled with either a poor name or an employee or customer who will be disgruntled if his winning selection is ignored.

Brainstorming by a chosen group of interested, but not necessarily enlightened, parties is another favorite approach. In 1983, the management of the Oklahoma Osteopathic Hospital of Tulsa set up a committee to establish a hospital prepaid health care plan. At one of its meetings, the committee decided to select a name for the plan. As could be expected from a group of physicians and hospital administrators unprepared for such a task, the selected name HEALTH CARE CHOICE was a phrase composed of words very likely to have been used by other health plans. This first mistake was compounded by a failure to perform a thorough availability check for the name. Shortly after the plan was put into operation, HEALTH CARE CHOICE was sued for trademark infringement by Aetna Health Care Systems, Inc., the owner of the mark CHOICE for the same type of health coverage services. The trial court granted Aetna an injunction against the newcomer's use of the term CHOICE, three times its actual damages, court costs, and attorneys' fees.

In each of the cases just mentioned, the creation of corporate identities and the coining of brand names was done haphazardly, with little or no attempt to follow the rules that govern the legal protection of commercial names.

The few professionals in the field have traditionally practiced their trade only within the narrow premises of their respective backgrounds or specialties—marketing, linguistics, or research and development. With the bliss of ignorance or the blindness of an ivory tower mentality, many professionals propose names that overlook the criteria dictated by the pertinent disciplines, except, of course, their own. The advertising expert tends to select descriptive terms that cannot pass legal muster. The linguist coins pleasant words that lack commercial impact. The R & D person may not see beyond the nuts and bolts of the product and may opt for a mark that belauds a technical feature, rather than an inspiring name that could catch the customer's attention.

Consequently, a vast majority of commercial names, (among the thousands chosen every day) are dull, difficult to recall, and often obstructive. Some even are legal time bombs that sooner or later will blow their users into the moil of infringement litigation. A small number of names are somewhat effective; an exceptional few are clearly outstanding. This last group owes more to chance than to knowledge or skill. As David Ogilvy once put it: "A blind pig can sometimes find truffles, but it helps to know that they are found in oak forests."

This book identifies and delineates the oak forest where the most flavorful truffles flourish. We first discuss the basic principles that govern the creation and use of commercial names and then define the techniques to coin truly effective ones. In doing so, we concentrate on the strength of three fundamental disciplines—marketing, semantics, and intellectual property law—with an honest attempt to translate some of their more abstruse principles and terminologies into concepts and terms intelligible to the small business owner and to the entrepreneur.

However, like every science, the creation of commercial names requires a special nomenclature. A glossary has been provided at the back of the book to acquaint you with a few neologisms introduced in this work and to serve as a convenient reference for certain traditional, but lesser known, technical terms.

Citations of relevant legal cases and statutes have also been compiled at the back of the book with cross-references to topics and names.

The characterization throughout the book of most customers, consumers, and other functionaries as men is intentional and does not imply the male gender. Such characterization invokes Webster's primary definition of man, namely "a human being; person, whether male or female," thus rendering unnecessary those depressing he/she and his/her routines.

If you have neither the time nor the inclination to create commercial names yourself, at least this book will enable you to make an informed criticism of the word-building efforts of others.

DEDICATION AND ACKNOWLEDGMENTS

"The Congress shall have Power to promote the Progress of Science and useful Arts," says Article I, Section 8 of the U.S. Constitution, "by securing for limited Times to Authors and Inventors the exclusive Right to their respective Writings and Discoveries." The federal patent and copyright statutes answer this mandate and provide the required incentives to authors, artists, and inventors.

I am convinced, however, that the ultimate goal expressed by the Founding Fathers can only be fulfilled by also providing a reward and incentive to those who bring the creations of those authors, artists, and inventors to the marketplace—the Entrepreneurs.

The most ingenious invention is of no benefit to the nation until it is brought into use in laboratories, offices, or factories, or made available to the public as a consumer product. The files of patent attorneys are encumbered with thousands of patents on wonderful creations and gadgets that have never effectively seen the light of day. In general, inventors make poor business people. In many cases, there is more merit in bringing a product to the market than there is in inventing it in the first place.

Is the Constitution unfair to entrepreneurs? Is there any legal incentive or reward for marketing savvy?

It took many years of dealing with enterprising individuals and fledgling businesses before I realized that there is indeed such a carrot implicit in our legal system, and that is the protection offered to distinctive commercial names. Names such as MACDONALD'S, MIDAS, and APPLE not only testify to the adventurous spirit and commercial acumen of certain enterprising individuals—they also are in themselves valuable commodities that can be lucratively exploited for many years to come. The law protects the establishment, expansion, and exploitation of such names for as long as they are used in commerce, providing that they meet certain basic criteria. Too many business people who introduce new products or create new firms miss that golden opportunity of developing an effective and valuable commercial name. Instead, they fetter their brainchild with a worthless or obtrusive moniker. It is therefore to the intrepid American entrepreneurs that I dedicate this book, along with the promise of financial reward and the avoidance of possible legal entanglements if they abide by its teachings.

It has taken me many years to synthesize the principles and methods in this book. Along the way, I have often benefited from the incisive advice of my associate, Arthur F. Holz, Esq., who will relive in its pages many of our spirited discussions. My mentor, F. C. Harding, who wields the sharpest pencil this side of the Pecos, has kept me within the bounds of acceptable English. And this book could not have been written without the patience, understanding, and encouragement of my loving Marcia. I must also reach way back in time and space to thank those who introduced me to the language—Monsieur Roussel and "Master" Bruni, e lei que me balhèron un nom, ont que siegan ara.

H. C.

The Name Is the Game
How to Name a Company or Product

PART 1

THE PRINCIPLES

Now I see what there is in a name; a word,
liquid, sane, unruly, musical, self-sufficient, . . .
Walt Whitman

CHAPTER 1

PRELIMINARIES

The art of naming companies, the products they manufacture, or the services they provide to their customers is called **semonemics**. This learned word from Greek—*semon* (identifier) and *semein* (to assign)—reflects the basic role fulfilled by commercial names—identification—and underscores the commercial and legal importance of the naming process. Few acts in the establishment of a commercial entity or the launching of a new product are as consequential for the success or failure of the enterprise as the assignment of the name under which that entity or product will be known in the marketplace. The main purpose of Part 1 is to convince you of that fact.

GOOD COMMERCIAL NAMES ARE NOT FOUND

The first thing you should know about good commercial names is that they are not fortuitously found. They almost never come to mind in a flash of inspiration. They cannot be collected from a crowd through naming contests. Instead, they must be built painstakingly from the ground up, piece by piece, in accordance with the rules of semonemics, taking into account all the marketing facts and legal factors that can be gathered and analyzed. This process is the subject of Part 2. You will learn how semonemics scientifically creates effective commercial names by eschewing arbitrary or subjective, and consequently unreliable, approaches in favor of a structured methodology. Without further ado, let us preview what should be found in a good commercial name.

A NAME IS A PROMISE

A name is a goodwill ambassador, a herald, a promise, the first thing that a consumer hears about a firm or its product. That first contact often determines the consumer's attitude toward the firm or product that the name identifies.

In the old days, most goods were sold unpackaged. The grocer would dispense flour or sugar by the ounce or the pound from large, unbranded barrels or other bulk containers. The customer could see, touch, or even taste the product before buying it. Symptomatically, the first California trademark statute enacted in 1861 only provided for registration of marks used in connection with bottled substances, bottles being the oldest and most enduring form of branded packages.

Nowadays, few goods are sold in bulk. Most products are presented in sealed packages. The buyer relies primarily on the brand name as a guarantee of quality and fitness. In this context, commercial names assume a critical role in the marketing of goods and services and in their acceptance by the public. The name endows the product with character, personality, and distinction to make the product acceptable or even desirable to the consumer. A company operating under an inappropriate identity is like a door hung with a misaligned hinge. It cannot work efficiently. A product branded with a poor mark is comparable to a plane equipped with the wrong set of wings. The thing may never fly. Furthermore, as is explained in Chapter 2, well-chosen commercial names can constitute a highly valuable commodity that can be independently and lucratively exploited.

DEFINITIONS

The names in question are those used in commerce—the names seen on signs and letterheads, the ones that are advertised in the media. These names can be classified into three broad categories.

A name that identifies a firm, whether it is a corporation, a partnership, or a sole proprietorship, as, for example, GENERAL MOTORS CORPORATION, is called a **trade name**.

The brand names under which that firm advertises and sells its products, such as CORVETTE, CHEVELLE, or IMPALA, are called **trademarks**.

If the firm is engaged in rendering services to the public rather than, or in addition to, selling goods, the name under which those services are promoted and rendered is called a **service mark**. For example, MR GOODWRENCH is a service mark for automotive maintenance services provided by the GENERAL MOTORS CORPORATION.

The principles and methods of name selection or creation that are explained in this book are equally applicable to the three categories of commercial names.

THE MECHANICS OF COMMERCIAL NAMES

The primary function of a trade name, trademark, or service mark is to identify; in other words, to distinguish a firm from other firms or the firm's products or services from those of competitors. Accordingly, a commercial name, whether it is a single word, a combination of two or more terms, or even an entire sentence, must be distinctive; that is, it must be original and unique. Distinctiveness is, in fact, the most important attribute of a name, from which the name derives its marketing value, effectiveness, and legal strength. More is said about this subject later.

As a primer, let us first analyze how a commercial name operates. The mind responds to two separate aspects of a name: its *impression* and its *meaning*.

The impression left by a name is what a psychologist would call the **engram**; namely, the impact the name has on the mind independent of the designated person or object. This would entail what a person would perceive upon hearing or reading an unfamiliar word for the first time—the pattern of letters forming that word, the sounds that the person hears or assigns to it in his own mind, and the emotive images that those letters and sounds conjure—what we colloquially could call the "drift" of the name.

The mention of the phrase "jingle bells" immediately brings to mind Christmas-card scenes of snowflakes, pine trees, and a bearded Santa Claus. These scenes are accompanied by a festive feeling and maybe some happy childhood memories. Those impressions are raised even before the literal meaning of the term is actually acknowledged or before ringing bells are visualized.

By contrast, the conventional or dictionary meaning of a noun is only a small part of the total message that noun conveys to our senses. It is limited to the known nature and attributes of the designated person or object.

The meaning of a commercial name is the identity, status, and reputation of the named company, or the nature and quality of some article of manufacture. But this is only part of the picture. The impression created by a commercial name may go far beyond this identifying role to bring to mind a variety of sensations. The creation of a commercial name must take into account the impression/meaning dichotomy and utilize the whole semantic power of words to reach the heart, as well as the mind, of the consumer.

The most desirable commercial name is one whose impression and meaning are perfectly tuned. It will be demonstrated how this synergistic combination can yield a more incisive and more memorable vocable.

The impression created by a word depends upon the sounds of its syllables and the pattern of its characters. Let us examine a couple of words that include what phoneticians call plosive guttural or dental consonants, for example, *garkon* and *stangor*. Although these words might be meaningless to us, they do nevertheless suggest strength, aggressiveness, and masculinity. Our language performs this type of phonetic stunt with such words as *tiger* and *cougar* to convey the ferocity of these animals. In those two terms, as Alexander Pope once said, the sound seems an echo to the sense. There is a coincidence between their respective impressions and meanings.

Let us go one step further. We can give new meanings to *tiger* and *cougar* by using them as commercial names or trademarks for such products as automobiles. In doing so, we have shifted to the impression side of the words and given them new meanings—a couple of highly individual sports cars. By the same token, the now-branded TIGER and COUGAR vehicles are suddenly endowed in the mind of the potential buyer with the qualities of swiftness and endurance proverbially attributed to the wild cats, in addition to the aggressive and thoroughly masculine image already conveyed by the hard-sounding syllables. The new meaning of those brand names is a reflection of the sounds originally conveyed by the borrowed words. This coordinated impact of sound and image to enhance the significance of a name constitutes a synergistic **sympiptism** (from the Greek *sumpiptein,* to coincide), something that, with all due credit to Al Capp, could be called a semantic double whammy! This mechanism is illustrated in Figure 1–1.

FIGURE 1–1
The mechanics of sympiptism.

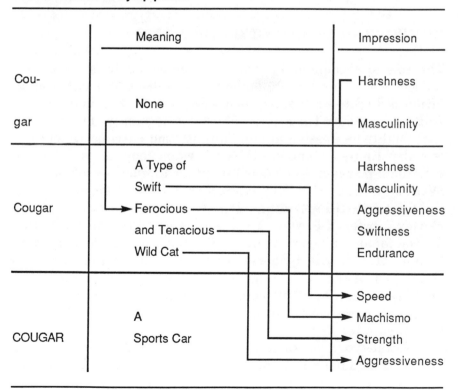

The judicious use of both the impression and meaning of words to enhance the power of a commercial name is one of the basic techniques of semonemics. A computer, no matter how well programmed, could not apply the simple sympiptic process to select or create effective identifiers. Like many other naming techniques discussed in this book, that process requires the artful touch of a well-informed technician.

The COUGAR example should give you a glimpse into the process of forming expressive commercial names with borrowed words. Another example, but with an opposite semantic effect, can be seen in the name Silk used to convey the softness and iridescence of a cosmetic product. Notice the combined effects of the soft *s* and *l* sounds with the lustrous image conjured by the word *silk*. This basic word-borrowing method of commercial name formation is developed through various simple techniques in Part 2 of this book.

BORROWING OR COINING THE NAME

The role of a commercial name-maker would be an easy one indeed if he could simply borrow names from the rich compilation of highly expressive terms found in a dictionary of the English language. The sad truth is that the supply of terms with such highly expressive latent contents and extrinsic meanings is rather limited. Gone are the days when companies and products could be readily identified by plain English words, such as IVORY or GREYHOUND—names that were often inspired by the most trivial happenings. It is said that, in or about 1879, Harley Procter of Procter & Gamble selected the name IVORY for the famous buoyant white soap upon hearing a sermon on Psalms XLV, 8: "All thy garments smell of myrrh and aloes and cassia, out of the ivory palaces whereby they have made thee glad." How quaint and uncomplicated things were in those days. The even more casual origin of the name GREYHOUND is recounted later.

Nowadays, most English words have already been used by others as commercial names. Close to a million marks are already registered with the U.S. Patent and Trademark Office. The only word-building components that remain generally available to the name-maker are expressive word fragments and etymological roots from which he must coin new terms. This is how such brand names as LUCITE, NYQUIL, and STARION are created, utilizing another semonemic process that is also analyzed in Part 2 of this book.

A ROSE NAMED SLIME WOULD NOT SELL WELL

As is explained later, the value, effectiveness, and incisiveness of a commercial name relate not to its ability to describe a company and its products, but rather to its ability to convey a positive and motivating message about the company and its products to the public.

A new commercial name, when heard for the first time, acts upon our mind only by means of its impression, without any reference to the firm or product it purports to identify. Once the liaison has been made between the name and the company or the product it designates, the mind attempts to establish a definite link between the two. To be effective (that is, memorable and motivating), the name should be attuned to its object. Shakespeare notwithstanding, a rose named SLIME, no matter how sweet smelling, would not sell well. The word SLIME has a very negative impression that, when associated with something as beautiful as a rose, can spoil the mental image of the rose's virtues. Indeed, a bad name can break a company or condemn its product to oblivion. On the other hand, a common and ordinary product can be made very attractive by branding it with a pleasant and very evocative name. An ordinary bar of soap assumes an aura of pleasure when it is sold under the mark CARESS. A roll of toilet paper acquires instant distinction when it is named CHARMIN.

Conveying the right message is the first rule of semonemics. It is explained later how that message is first formulated and then translated into a name.

WATCH YOUR LANGUAGE

You must remember that a name may not carry the same message for everybody. As the linguist Mario Pei observed, "a word or sentence is not merely a sound; it is also a bundle of associations . . . . no two individuals derive precisely the same shade of meaning out of the same utterance." Each individual reacts to a name in his own way, which is dictated by his background and experience. To most Americans, the brand name SHASTA immediately conjures the refreshing image of a snow-covered mountain. Europeans not so familiar with the U.S. landscape may only hear in that word a fizzing sound. The effects on both groups of people are actually very positive, and particularly evocative and motivating when the name is used to identify a brand of soda pop. This may not always be the case. A particular name may trigger a very positive response in one person but some very unpleasant feelings in another. It is therefore imperative to select or create commercial names that fit not only the nature of the product but also the profile of the consumer. This match-making process is explained in greater length in several later chapters. Numerous examples will demonstrate that the most effective names are those that are designed primarily to please the prospective customer.

AN ART AND A SCIENCE

A commercial name that identifies a company or distinguishes the company's products from others must be unique and original, yet capable of carrying a favorable message to motivate the customer toward having dealings with that company. Creating such a name is an art, as well as a science, with rules and guidelines rooted in sociology, psychology, semantics, and last but not least, the law.

Sociology and psychology help us to analyze the typical consumer and tell us what he likes to hear in a name, as well as what terms or sounds may favorably predispose him toward a particular product or service. Semantics teaches us how to communicate the intended message or how to impart a certain thought in the mind of the targeted audience. The laws concerning commercial names and unfair competition define the proprietary rights that can attach to a trade name, trademark, or service mark to prevent its misappropriation by others. A name might be pleasant and highly motivating, but if no proprietary right attaches to it, this spells danger. Its very success will make the name a tempting prey for competitors, who by adopting the very same name will take along all the goodwill and reputation that the first user has painstakingly built into it. When a court of law dismisses the claim of a frustrated plaintiff who thought he was riding a thoroughbred of a name, the plaintiff may discover that, in fact, he has mounted his business on the back of a bucking bronco. Such commercial names as:

SUPER GLUE	for an adhesive
READER	for a newspaper
LITE	for a low-calorie beer
WINDSURFER	for sailboards
SAFARILAND	for a clothing store
BUILDERS EMPORIUM	for a building supply shop
COMPUTER STORE	for a computer dealer outlet

just to name a few, are examples of names that courts found to be unworthy of legal protection and that have been freely copied as a result.

Being copied is not the worst that can befall the user of a haphazardly selected name. The sheer multitude of legally protectable vocables already in use creates a densely packed legal minefield. The careless intruder will soon be blown to bits by a burst of costly infringement lawsuits.

Legal considerations are therefore primordial in naming a company or a product. As will be amply illustrated throughout this book, legal requirements, far from being constraining, work hand in hand with market-oriented criteria to help the name-maker in carrying out his work safely and effectively. Moreover, creativity is most effective when properly channeled. Semonemics with its multifaced discipline can provide the hearth as well as the fuel for your creative fire which otherwise would burn aimlessly and unproductively to exhaustion.

CHAPTER 2

THE ROLE OF COMMERCIAL NAMES

Before we can define a complete methodology for the creation of a commercial name, we must first have a clear understanding of the role that such a name fulfills in the field of business. That role is threefold:

1. To promote the products or services of a company
2. To protect against copycat imitations and other unfair appropriations
3. To generate profit when exercised or traded by its owner

The degree of promotion, protection, and profit that can be derived from the use of a commercial name depends almost entirely upon the intrinsic characteristics of the syllables, words, and phrases that make that name. If a name is distinctive and appealing, it will be easily remembered and will effectively motivate the customer. Its uniqueness and appeal will advantageously position the product or service on the market. The distinctiveness of the name translates into legal clout, which in turn helps in protecting that market position. As the name gathers strength and reputation, it becomes a valuable commodity that can be lucratively exploited.

PROMOTION

A good name should motivate the individual who hears it into buying the product or service it identifies, or steer the potential customer toward the company that uses it as its trade name.

The mark SHASTA, with its refreshing allusion to the snow-covered peak, can bring refreshment into the mind of the already thirsty individual and motivate him into buying the soft drink it designates.

Imagine a traveling businesswoman who arrives in a big city for a very important interview. She needs to have her hair professionally "done." She picks up a telephone directory to look for a convenient beauty shop, and she spots two listings for the nearby area. One is named ROMANCE STYLISTS; the other is called ERNIE'S SALON. Being from out of town, the lady has no idea about the reputation of either one of those two businesses. However, chances are that she will, rightly or wrongly, select the classy-and-romantic-sounding listing and give poor Ernie the cold shoulder. The owner of the ROMANCE STYLISTS shop has gained another customer, thanks to the impression projected by the shop's service mark.

Once a customer has experienced and appreciated the quality of a product sold under a particular trademark, when faced again with a choice between that brand and several other similar products, he will quite naturally return to the first one. Names that have acquired favorable meanings, based on the customer's experience of the quality and reputation of the products or services they identify, guide the consumer into repurchasing those same products or services. Sometimes, the consumer's preference is not based on personal experience with the product, but on the recommendation of another or on the consumer's response to a good publicity campaign. In either case, it is the label that directs the consumer to the goods. Products branded with a mark that leaves a highly motivating impression may promote themselves with little publicity. Products sold under a less inspiring name must, instead, rely for promotion upon their own merits or on a well-orchestrated advertising campaign.

When a new product is launched under a unique and inspiring handle, the product acquires an extremely advantageous position on the market. This position may be impregnable if the subsequent competition cannot use the name under which the product first appeared or another closely similar term. That initial positioning contributes not only to the promotion of the product but also to the product's protection, as is explained in the next section.

PROTECTION

When one talks about protecting a product, the first thing that usually comes to mind is a patent. However, the percentage of products on the market that are protected by patent is relatively low, compared to products that derive their exclusivity from a strong name.

A name acts as a protection for a product in two basic ways. First, as already mentioned, it positions the product on the market against the competition. Anybody who introduces a new product has the opportunity to give it a protected name, that is, a trademark that nobody else can use. The public exposed to that new product under that particular name will, if the name is fitting and memorable, forever associate the name with that kind of product. Once the consumer is used to calling this type of product by the proprietary name, he will tend to ignore similar products offered by other companies under less familiar designations.

There are articles that most of us will not buy except under their original brand names, such as FORMICA, VELCRO, and KODAK. There are other brands of laminated plastic veneers, hook-and-vane fabric fasteners, and photographic films on the market, but they are dominated by the previously named goods. This is because the strong names selected by the original manufacturers have elevated those goods on the market and in the mind of the consumer to an outstanding position. Other manufacturers of the same or similar products cannot use those dominant names and are consequently fettered by a tremendous handicap.

Furthermore, having favorably positioned an article on the market, a strong name protects the product against unfair competition. The misappropriation of a trade name, trademark, or service mark, or the use of a confusingly similar term is prohibited by law. Such acts can be enjoined by restraining orders, sometimes accompanied by seizure and destruction of the counterfeit goods. Commercial names can be recorded with the U.S. Customs Service, which will then confiscate imported goods bearing one of those recorded names without the control or consent of the name's lawful owner.

Entrepreneurs and companies seeking to introduce a new product onto the market should never underestimate the broad and easily enforceable protection that they may derive from the use of a strong name in addition to, or in lieu of, the not so easily enforced protection afforded by patents. The protective role attributable to distinctive commercial names has not been fully appreciated by the legal community and in particular by the intellectual property specialists. Is it any wonder that business and marketing people are, in general, unaware of the extent of protection that can be obtained from the selection of a defensible moniker? A fledgling company on a tight budget and in need of effective protection for its new product should consider the creation of a good name. This might be more appropriate, and in the long run more effective, than a patent application in placing the product in a better competitive position. In most cases, patents take years and large expenditures of money before they are granted. They are difficult to enforce, even after months of expensive litigation. They require a public disclosure of the goods or of their method of manufacture, and they have a limited life. Trademarks, by contrast, can be readily created, are valid as long as they are used, and can be expeditiously enforced through summary proceedings, as is demonstrated in Chapter 5. Although a trademark is no substitute for a good patent, where a patent is duly indicated, under the proper circumstances, a distinctive name might offer just the right degree of protection necessary to effectively propel the product or service to a secure market position.

PROFIT

In ancient Egypt, names were believed to have an existence separate from the person or thing they designated. Commercial names have made this belief a reality in the modern marketplace. Not only do commercial names have an existence of their own, but they constitute assets of great monetary value. That value can be converted into hard cash, upon the sale of the business or even earlier, if the name is exploited through a licensing, merchandising, or franchising program.

Every time you buy a product, you probably pay something for the names that appear on the label—the trade name of the manufacturer and the trademark of the product. That is because manufacturers and sellers who offer an article or product that has acquired a good reputation can ask a higher price than the customer would pay for an article or product of the same type sold under an unknown label. One could argue that the customer pays a higher price not because of the names that appear on the package but because of the reputation enjoyed by the product itself or by its maker. This may be so, but that reputation cannot be carried except by a legally strong name that nobody else can use. If other companies could use the same name, its appearance on the label would no longer be a guaranty of quality. The buyer would no longer be sure that what he is getting comes from that particular, highly reputable firm or that the article is of the same quality as the one he has satisfactorily used before.

Actually, many products are not made by their original manufacturer. Most products nowadays are made by various unrelated firms using the same trademark under license from the original manufacturer. For example, a polo shirt sold under the HANG TEN name may have been manufactured by any one of the many licensees of the Hang Ten International. Similarly, services can be rendered under the same mark by independent establishments under a franchise agreement.

Licenses and franchises are legal contractual arrangements. Under these, the manufacturer of a product or the provider of a service to the general public authorizes other firms to make and sell the product or to render the services under the name or mark developed by the licensor or franchisor. In other words, licensing and franchising are methods for leasing a name for use by others. This type of contractual relationship often includes some transfer of know-how and technical assistance on the part of the originator of the name.

In the United States, one-third of all retail sales involves some sort of franchise, and one out of every seven persons is connected to a business operating under a franchise. As the service sector of the U.S. economy continues to outgrow the manufacturing sector, the exploitation of service marks through franchise contracts will continue to expand. Many franchising schemes are strictly based on the leasing of a name, with little or no transfer of technology or assistance from the franchisor to his franchisees. Indeed, low-technology industries, such as fast food, dry cleaning, or automobile services, differ little in the types and degrees of services they offer to their customers. There are few or no special skills required to fry a hamburger, scoop out ice cream, or detail an automobile. Thus, we can safely conclude that the fees paid by the franchisee to the franchisor, which are usually based on a percentage of gross sales, are basically rent payments for the use of an exclusive name and not consideration for any substantial amount of technical assistance.

Certain names are so strong, so highly visible, and so readily accepted by the public that they can be rented for use on a wide variety of goods, sometimes totally unrelated to the original use of the name. This form of licensing, sometimes called **merchandising,** is based strictly on the value of the name itself, on its impression rather than its meaning. The names PLAYBOY, YVES SAINT LAURENT, and SERGIO VALENTE appear on a multitude of products, from garments and perfumes to sporting goods and housewares. Merchandising is name exploitation par excellence. Even the fashion-conscious lady who buys a shopping bag graced with the signature of YVES SAINT LAURENT knows very well that the famous couturier had very little, if anything, to do with the design of that bag. SERGIO VALENTE is a made-up mark, yet customers are willing to pay extra money for any product adorned with that name.

One can even say that commercial names constitute the most traded commodity. First, because every product and every company has a name, and every time products are sold or services are rendered under that company name, part of the price paid by the customer is for the name. In the case where the merchant is a licensee or a franchisee, the price reflects, in part, the fees paid to the owner of that name.

Commercial names are also traded—that is, bought and sold. This occurs when the assets of a company change hands. Those assets usually comprise buildings, equipment, stock-in-trade, and an intangible called goodwill. Goodwill, in fact, is the reputation of the company, its relationship with its customers, most of which is embodied in the company's trade name and trademarks. There is a tax advantage for the seller of a going business in defining the goodwill in terms of trade names and trademarks or service marks, rather than as "ongoing business" or "future earnings capability." A concern saddled with a weak or nontransferable name, such as the seller's surname, may not be able to justify a high goodwill value.

Finally, you should realize that commercial names are also traded on the stock market, just as any other type of commodity. When an investor buys twenty shares of XEROX CORPORATION, it is understood that what he is buying is a small fraction of that company ownership and all the rights attached to it, including the right to receive dividends out of the company profit. Many speculators buy stock in a company, not because they are interested in ownership per se or because they expect some future dividends, but because they are responding to the popularity of the stock and are counting on an increase in value in the near future. They may not know anything about the company, its management, or its product line. These investors rely strictly on the name and the past performance of that name on the stock market.

Recently, a small, relatively unknown retail furniture dealer, whose stock was quoted on the over-the-counter market, changed its name from THE BRICK WAREHOUSE to the more inspiring trade name FURNISHING 2000. Five days after the announcement of the name change, the stock of that company went up 30 percent, although nothing had happened internally to justify that sudden increase in stock value except the name change.

The same happy result occurred when INDUSTRIAL NATIONAL CORPORATION changed its name to FLEET FINANCIAL GROUP. "We are followed a lot more closely by Wall Street" noted its vice-president for marketing and advertising. The corporate identity change of the concern formerly known as CONSOLIDATED FOODS to SARA LEE was, according to one of its vice-presidents, prompted by a desire to increase the value of its stock and to increase awareness of the corporation. Within twelve months from the name change, the stock of the company doubled in value.

These anecdotes vividly demonstrate the value of a good name and the power and influence it can have upon those of the general public who come in contact with it.

At the start of a new business or upon the introduction of a new product to the market, there is offered to the well-advised business person a chance to create value out of nothing by selecting or creating a good name. Yet, the majority of companies and products are named without any attempt to create a distinctive and motivating trade name or trademark that could provide good promotion, protection, and most of all, substantial profit.

CHAPTER 3

NAMES TO AVOID

Certain categories of names for various and diverse reasons do not make good commercial names. It makes sense to clear the air at this time by listing those categories and pointing out the defects in the names. This should leave you free to focus on the selection and creation of truly effective identifiers, unencumbered by preconceived false notions. The names to be avoided are personal surnames, definitions, names already used by others, initials, and terms having inappropriate homonyms or translations.

PRIDE OF THE PEACOCK

By far, the most common mistake made when naming a new company is to name it after its founder. The Yellow Pages Directories are replete with listings the like of SMITH BROTHERS, INC., SMITH COMMUNICATIONS, JONES & SONS, JONES MORTGAGES, or JONES INDUSTRIES. Whether because of pride or vanity, many entrepreneurs cannot resist the temptation of christening their firms with their own family name.

To be effective in the marketplace, a name must be distinctive and, if possible, unique. There is in most cases nothing distinctive about patronyms. Even if a person is blessed with a highly unusual and memorable name, to make it part of a trade name shows very little foresight. What will happen, for instance, if the company is sold? The new buyer may not want to operate under the seller's name. The seller himself may find it difficult to part with something as personal as his own family name. He may be concerned that any bad performance by the buyer under his name may reflect adversely upon his personal reputation. If a business, on the other hand, is forced to change name upon sale, it may lose a substantial part of the goodwill acquired under the prior identity. Worse, if there is no name transfer, there may be nothing upon which to hang the goodwill. Accordingly, the Internal Revenue Service may treat any portion of the sale proceeds attributed to goodwill as partial compensation for loss of future earnings, therefore as capital gain. Normally, the transfer of a trade name would qualify for capital gain treatment. However, the tax courts have ruled that an individual cannot completely divest himself of his own name and have refused to treat proceeds from such attempted transfers as capital gain. The characterization of proceeds as ordinary income rather than capital gain may result in an unexpected tax liability to the seller. If the consideration for the sale of the business is not paid in cash but with a promissory note or an exchange of assets, the seller may be unable to meet his tax obligations at year end. The Tax Reform Act of 1986 did away with the 60 percent long-term capital gain deduction for noncorporate taxpayers but did not change the character of gain or loss from capital to ordinary. Long-term capital gains can still be offset against long-term losses. In view of the new restrictions applied to the transfer of those losses to the buyer in the sale of a business, they can only be offset against the sale proceeds if these proceeds qualify as capital gain. If the proceeds of the sale are treated as ordinary income, the accumulated losses may be lost forever. Vanity in naming can be costly.

There are many other potential problems with businesses operating under a family name. Who retains the name when the Smith brothers no longer see eye to eye and decide to split the firm? Once Mr. Taylor has sold his TAYLOR winery, name, stock, and barrels, can he himself go back into the wine business? How about his children or his nieces and nephews bearing the same surname—can they open another TAYLOR winery? Those situations lead to expensive litigations and ugly family feuds.

Naming a product or a service after an individual also has some unhappy consequences. The Lanham Act, the federal statute that regulates the protection of marks and other designations of origin, states that marks that are merely family surnames and names of individuals are not registrable. The importance of a Lanham Act registration is discussed in Chapter 15. It suffices to say at this time that registrability of a brand name or service mark is one of the first goals in name selection and creation.

Except in those rare instances where the name of an individual has already acquired notoriety, as, for example, YVES SAINT LAURENT, a surname, whether it is the name of the firm founder or that of another individual, should be avoided in the naming of a company or its products.

One of the most challenging tasks that a name-maker working for a medical appliance manufacturer may face is to convince a physician who has developed a new medical device that traditional eponymic designations should be forfeited for the benefit of more enlightened names. If Dr. Able and Dr. Doe have developed a more effective splint, they will expect to see it marketed as the ABLE-DOE splint and not under a coined name. However, eponyms are marred with most of the same latent defects that afflict other types of commercial patronyms— they are uninspiring, lack distinctiveness, and cannot be protected.

As the practice of medicine is becoming more competitive, the attitude of physicians is changing. Practices that not long ago physicians considered crass commercialism are now becoming quite acceptable to the profession. Improvements in surgical procedures that yesterday were routinely disclosed in professional journals for free use by other practitioners are now patented and exploited through royalty-bearing licenses. University professors and scientists do not hesitate to join the staffs of biomedical and bioengineering firms. These firms are more efficient in taking medical breakthroughs out of the laboratory and into the market than are the universities and can return handsome financial rewards. The commercial realities that revolutionized the practice of medicine also require that eponyms give way to impersonal trademarks in the commercialization of medical appliances and other products.

DEFINITIONS

If you open a Yellow Pages Directory, you will find under the "plumbers" heading many names, such as AFFORDABLE PLUMBING, DAY AND NIGHT PLUMBERS, or CONSOLIDATED PLUMBING. These are not particularly memorable or inspiring names and are hard to distinguish from one another. The problem with these listings is that they are not using names but definitions.

A name is meant to identify, that is, to distinguish one person from another, one object from the next. The best identifying name is a unique word used to designate a single individual or single company. The names EXXON and KODAK very distinctively identify an oil company and a brand of photographic products.

A definition, on the other hand, is meant to indicate the type, quality, attributes, or function of the person or object in question. "Oil company" and "photographic products" are generic phrases that could apply to various firms engaged in the petroleum and photographic equipment industries. Definitions of like products or services tend to sound alike. They cannot be distinctive.

The law, mindful of the difference between names and definitions, acknowledges and even protects the monopolization of a distinctive name by its first user but cannot permit the monopolization of a definition. The reason is that to reserve for someone the exclusive use of a unique name does not take anything away from anybody else. By contrast, the monopolization of a word or phrase that defines something would deprive the rest of us from the use of that part of the language and cannot be tolerated. Accordingly, the degree of protection accorded to a trade name or to a mark depends upon the level of distinctiveness and, by corollary, the lack of descriptiveness exhibited by that name or mark. The more descriptive the name, the more difficult it will be to prevent its use by others. This is the golden rule of commercial names protection and the first and foremost criterion in the selection and creation of those names. The problem with the bad names cited in the last section of Chapter 1 is that they are too descriptive.

There are various degrees of descriptiveness, and the worst case consists of naming a company or a product by the generic term, that is, the common word or words used to define the activity of the company or the nature of the product.

A pencil manufacturer could not sell his wares under the mark PENCIL and hope to prevent any other manufacturer of pencils from using that name. Yet, this is exactly what many companies try to do, as narrated every week in the reports of important court decisions.

The cases revolving around the mark LITE, which was listed as one of the poorest name choices in Chapter 1, are worth some further comments at this time. In the early 1970s, the Miller Brewing Company of Milwaukee, Wisconsin, one of the largest purveyors of beer in the United States, spent a considerable amount of money developing a process to reduce the calorie count in beer and came up with a new type of brew.

At that time, the famous brewery had a golden opportunity to create a strong name for the new beverage that would help in positioning the product on the market and give it a good head start by denying the competition the use of that first name, just like FORMICA did as a highly distinctive mark for laminated plastic veneers. Let us imagine, for the sake of argument, that the low-calorie brew had been introduced to the market by Miller Brewing Company under the brand CHAMP. This may not be the most appropriate name for this kind of beverage, but it is one that is fanciful and fairly distinctive. With a little promotion, CHAMP could have soon become a popular name almost synonymous with low-calorie beer. The competition would have been forced to spend a great deal in reconditioning the public to buy the same product under another name. If they did not succeed, CHAMP may have gained and maintained a dominating position similar to the one still held after forty years by FORMICA in the laminated plastic field.

Let us return to reality. The famous brewery selected the term LITE for its new product. This term is legally equivalent to the word *light,* which, as the courts ruled later, is a generic or common descriptive term when used in connection with a low-calorie beverage and is so clearly unprotectible that no amount of advertising or promotion could salvage it. Miller did spend great sums of money in promoting its LITE beer, only to see its competitors—Heileman Brewing Company, Falstaff Brewing Corporation, Rainier Brewing Company, Joseph Schlitz Brewing Company, and a few others—adopt the LITE or LIGHT name brand. The multitude of expensive litigations that resulted were concluded in favor of the defendants. The most significant loss was not the expense of those futile lawsuits but the missed golden opportunity to establish a strong market position for a new brew, one heartily welcomed by weight-conscious beer drinkers.

Miller's gaffe had some very broad repercussions. Once the term LITE or LIGHT was established and accepted as synonymous with "low-calorie count," it was heavily exploited by certain cola makers. They were able to use such brands as PEPSI LIGHT to erode the prominent posture acquired by Coca-Cola Company in the field of diet sodas under its highly distinctive mark TAB.

The name COCA-COLA itself provides us with another illustration of the insidious and long-lasting consequences of choosing a descriptive name. COCA-COLA is indeed a very effective mark, due to its strong aural impact. Its popularity, however, owes more to the tremendous amount of promotion dollars that the Atlanta company has put behind it for many years than to the inherent character of the name itself. Frank M. Robinson, an associate of Dr. John Styth Pemberton, the originator of the drink, composed the famous brand in 1886 by combining the names of the drink's principal ingredients—coca leaves and kola nut extracts. If COCA-COLA was not such a descriptive mark, the competition would not have been allowed to adopt such names as PEPSI COLA or RC COLA. To this day, every time the Coca-Cola Company, with its massive advertising campaigns, opens a new market in a developing country, it is paving the way for its freeloading competitors, who can use the word *cola* as part of their own names. The promotion of the name COKE was somewhat of an attempt to limit the damages. Since the coca leaf is no longer part of the syrup formula, the names COCA and COKE are no longer descriptive in connection with the product and are therefore protectible. The word *cola* has such a following that a certain company, which does not use the extract in its soda, employs *cola* in its advertising slogan by calling its drink "THE UN-COLA" which is a very subtle (even perhaps unintentional) way to ride on the coattails of the Atlanta giant.

The rule thus appears to be very simple: avoid descriptive or generic terms. Yet, it is clear from the weekly case reports that the mistakes of Miller Brewing Company and Coca-Cola's Mr. Robinson are repeated over and over again. The enterprising company that pioneered a very refreshing drink of wine and citrus juice very unwisely branded the product WINE COOLER. It could not protect that choice of name and made it quite easy for its competitors to capture a good portion of its clientele by using the term *cooler* on their own labels. The Joseph Coors Brewing Company was no better inspired when it decided to call its version of wine cooler WINE CHILLER.

This stubborn preference for descriptive names indicates that their promoters select the names on the basis of the name's informative value, without consideration of the marketing and legal consequences. It may be that very few names are selected or coined by marketing experts or by trademark practitioners but instead are created by what may be called **technicians.** These are mainly manufacturers who remain obsessed by the functional aspects and qualities of the goods rather than the needs, tastes, and motivation of potential buyers. These technicians take the perhaps short-sighted and sometimes narrow-minded view that their companies or products should primarily be known by what they are, what they do, or how they do it. They do not realize that such descriptive or generic names are flawed by two serious marketing weaknesses:

1. They are indistinguishable from similar terms that are already used or are soon to be used by the competition.
2. They expose the goodwill accumulated by the company to easy capture by competitors.

Let us go back to the Yellow Pages and the listing of computer equipment dealers. We can find several trade names, such as COMPUTER STORE, COMPUTER MERCHANT, COMPUT-ERLAND, COMPUTER MART, etc., which are mutually indistinguishable. In addition, most of the computer manufacturers who pioneered the minicomputer revolution and later the microcomputer invasion carried some very descriptive corporate

identities: DIGITAL EQUIPMENT CORPORATION, CON-
TROL DATA CORPORATION, DATA GENERAL CORPORA-
TION, and so on. Most people find this mumbojumbo of technical
terms very confusing and difficult to remember. As a result, the
well-meaning promotional purpose that initially dictated the
selection of those names is totally negated by the confusion resulting from the proliferation of sound-alikes.

By contrast, in the early 1980s, an innovative company broke
away from the pack by adopting a highly distinctive name—
APPLE. The rest is history. The word APPLE carries no descriptive or generic sense when applied to computers. For that
reason, it makes a strikingly unique trade name and trademark,
whose stature extends clearly above the names of the computer
manufacturers named earlier. The phenomenal success of AP-
PLE computers was not solely due to the quality of the product.
Experts agree that there were, at the time, some better machines
already on the market. However, the name APPLE was so re-
freshingly new, so attractive to the consumer, and so easily protectible it positioned the new product very favorably on the
market against the older companies. Can anyone believe that
such a success story would have been possible if, instead of AP-
PLE, the maverick company had adopted another descriptive
run-of-the-mill name, such as DIGITAL CONTROL CORPO-
RATION or COMPUTER DATA COMPANY?

The franchisor of the COMPUTERLAND chain of computer
dealerships was not too pleased when a similar chain of stores be-
gan expanding under the name MICROLAND. Claims for public
confusion and misappropriation of goodwill were brought against
the newcomer, but to no avail. The court found the name COM-
PUTERLAND too descriptive to deserve an aura of protection so
broad as to cover a name like MICROLAND. The user of the
BUILDERS EMPORIUM name for a building supply store once
attempted to prevent the operation of an unrelated company under the very same name. He lost the resulting lawsuit. Adopting
a name identical or similar to that of a successful business may be
done with impunity if that name is descriptive and has not yet
acquired a degree of notoriety and association with a single source
or ownership. The rule of law cannot be expressed better than did
the court in the BUILDERS EMPORIUM case, which stated:

"As a matter of law, one may not obtain a proprietary interest in a title or name merely by formulating the same words in the English language and thereafter using it in connection with an enterprise. Despite a persistent belief that the first use of a specific name or description gives a power to such user to prevent its employment by others, it is important to find that no such doctrine exists. . . . Since, therefore, the name BUILDERS EMPORIUM is merely a highly descriptive name composed of words of common meaning generic in character, it is my conclusion that plaintiff could acquire no proprietary right to exclusive use thereof by mere priority of use. . . . In other words, mere priority of use of a name gives a plaintiff no rights in that name, unless he can also show that the public identified the name with the plaintiff's business prior to defendant adoption and use of the name."

THOU SHALT NOT STEAL

The adoption of a distinctive name that is already used by somebody else is to be avoided at all costs if there is any likelihood of confusion in the public mind as to the relationship of the parties or the origin of their goods or services. This, in a nutshell, is the law of the land regarding proprietary rights to distinctive commercial names. A trademark attorney should be retained to conduct a search and to render an opinion on the availability of the prospective name choice in connection with the name's contemplated use. Later on, we discuss what should be covered by such a search and opinion. At this point, it is emphasized that the search and also the opinion interpreting its results within the context of the contemplated use are both necessary. The result of a bare mechanical search, no matter how thorough it may be, can lead the untrained mind to false and dangerous conclusions. An availability search for a commercial name can be expensive, if conducted, as it should be, on a national scale or even with an international scope. Furthermore, if the name is found to be already preempted, the whole search process must be repeated around a new name candidate. Thus, reducing the risk of a later discovery of nonavailability can result in substantial savings.

This may begin to sound like a broken record, but the risk of conflict will greatly diminish if the prospective name is nondescriptive and inherently distinctive in the first place. In other words, one must stay clear of beaten paths. It is wiser to pick another APPLE than to look for a gap in the litanies of overused technical terms. Coining a new word such as ALPO for a dog food, instead of using English terms as was done with TENDER VITTLES, improves the odds in favor of availability. If you prefer to stick to English words, a vaguely suggestive mark like CHUCK WAGON is less likely to be already in use than the more descriptive TENDER VITTLES.

Of course, the main reasons for staying clear of names similar or too close to one already in use are: (1) to protect against claims of infringement or counterfeiting, (2) to avoid being subjected to injunctions and seizure orders, and (3) to avoid being forced to change one's identity after having already developed some goodwill and reputation under the infringing name.

There is another reason for staying clear of a name already in use by someone else, which, if not always obvious, is nevertheless as important as avoiding infringement. No businessman with pride in the quality of his products or services could tolerate seeing his competitor's products purchased in place of his by buyers confused by the similarity of names. Although a prospective name may not be so close to another as to constitute a legal infringement, the similarity of the two names may someday lead to detrimental confusion in the mind of the public. Selecting a very distinctive name is a good assurance against such occurrences.

ALPHABET SOUP

Frequently, a company is burdened with the surnames of long-departed founders or with a descriptive technical name that no longer fits its product line. In this situation, it is not unusual to resort to crunching of the cumbersome corporate identity down to an acronym or to initials. LING TEMKO VOUGHT became LTV, NATIONAL CASH REGISTER turned into NCR, and MIN-

NESOTA MINING AND MANUFACTURING metamorphosed into the 3M Company. The problem with this alphabet soup is that there are only so many letters to play with, so the chance of conflict, present or future, is very high. Furthermore, initials carry no message and therefore are neither memorable nor motivating. The courts, as a result, have been reluctant to allow a party to monopolize a pack of letters and enforce it against an imitator except in the most outrageous cases. A new business should therefore avoid the risk of drowning its reputation in that particular brand of soup.

SCARECROWS, SKELETONS, AND SCATOLOGY

The last category of names that should be avoided consists of those that may be perceived negatively or pejoratively by certain classes of people or those that might cast derision on their owners. Words that suggest death, suffering, and other painful evocations may sometimes creep into a commercial name. The word *pane* may be perceived as *pain* by some individuals. The name BIOVEST, which was applied to a biomedical venture capital firm, is phonetically too close to *biowaste*. You should therefore be wary of the homonyms of certain words either in English or in other languages. If a product is destined for a foreign market, you should make certain that the English name does not suggest something morbid, ridiculous, or obscene in the local idiom. In Japanese, the word *shi,* which means four, has the same pronunciation as the word for death. There is a parallel in Korean with the word *sa.* Both should be avoided in a name that might be exported to the Orient. The existence of a large Spanish-speaking population in the United States requires that all new choices of names be acceptable in that language. The name NOVA for an automobile, with a shift of accentuation, means "does not run" in several Romance languages. Those readers familiar with the French tongue will understand why such names as CAMELOT and CON EDISON are not exportable to many countries. Consider what risks might be run by the French bottlers of the highly popular PERRIER mineral water if they should dare to

import their long-established PSCHITT soda pop label into an English-speaking country!

In view of the ever-increasing importance of international trade and the vital necessity for American manufacturers to export abroad, all new commercial names should be checked carefully for compatibility with all markets where they may be introduced.

CHAPTER 4

ANATOMY OF A GOOD NAME

We have in the preceding chapters covered so much forbidden territory and so many taboos that you may be wondering what, if anything, is left out of which to forge a good commercial name. We cannot use generic terms and words already preempted by others. We should stay away from descriptive terms, family surnames, initials, any name that could be confused with existing ones, and those that may carry a bad connotation in English, Spanish, or the language of any other country where the name is to be used. What then could be left to use in forming a good commercial name for a company or for its products? The answer to that question is simple: plenty!

Before defining a method for selection or creation of commercial names and to help you in understanding the most important characteristics of such names, let us analyze a few outstanding ones.

GREYHOUND

The service mark GREYHOUND identifies the transportation services provided by several bus lines controlled by the GREYHOUND CORPORATION. The origin of the name has been the subject of a great deal of controversy, both in and out of court, between several claimants to the first use of GREYHOUND in the field of public transportation. According to one version, the name was adopted in the early 1920s by a Wisconsin bus service operator who was using two elongated touring cars. He is said to have been inspired by the innkeeper at the Fond du Lac,

Wisconsin, stop, who remarked that the cars looked "just like greyhounds."

The name GREYHOUND is highly distinctive because it has no direct descriptive relationship with the services it identifies. A dictionary definition of the word *Greyhound* is "a tall dog of the hound family remarkable for its swiftness in running." The term has also been applied to speedy ocean liners. Thus, the word gives an impression of celerity, in addition to the friendliness and fidelity attributed to dogs in general.

The name GREYHOUND promotes the services of the bus company by first being extremely easy to remember. The evocation of a gracefully speeding dog in connection with a bus line becomes permanently engraved in the customer's mind as soon as he hears the name GREYHOUND. That image will help in recalling the name whenever the customer is in need of transportation services.

The name GREYHOUND is highly distinctive because it has no direct descriptive relationship with the services it identifies. A dictionary definition of the word *greyhound* is "a tall dog of the hound family remarkable for its swiftness in running." The term has also been applied to speedy ocean liners. Thus, the word gives an impression of celerity, in addition to the friendliness and fidelity attributed to dogs in general.

successful in preventing the adoption of the name, not only by direct competitors but also by a stock brokerage house, GREYHOUND SECURITIES, INC. of New York. In that case, the court took judicial notice of the "primacy" of the name and of its unambiguous association by the general public with the plaintiff's services.

Because of all this, the name GREYHOUND is an important asset of the company that, should the company be sold, could carry its entire goodwill. The name could also be franchised or merchandised within the industry in exchange for fees or royalties.

This example tells us that a very eloquent and memorable commercial name can be created by using a word having no direct descriptive relationship to the nature or services of the named company. In this case, a word was used that was highly suggestive of the qualities (celerity, dependability) expected from such services. The empathy and emotions of the customer can also be heightened by using a word describing something dear, pleasant, and comforting. This was also done here by using the name of one of the friendliest and most faithful animals on earth. Thus, the name GREYHOUND strikes a pleasant chord in the heart of the customer, while conveying to the customer's mind some very desirable attributes. This powerful, multifaceted message cannot be found in a name such as TRAILWAYS, which was used for very much the same type of services.

JELLIBEANS

Turning now to a lesser known enterprise, let us analyze the name JELLIBEANS used as a service mark for a skating rink in Atlanta, Georgia. The mark is derived from a word that defines a type of colorful candy. Here again, there is no generic or descriptive connection between the selected name and the services provided by the company. The intrinsic value of the name comes from the fact that it describes something sweet, a favorite food of children. Thus, the name's first impression is pleasure. The name JELLIBEANS was wisely selected to appeal to the class of consumers who normally patronize a skating rink, that is, children. The unexpected association of a type of candy with a skating rink creates immediately an indelible impression on the minds of children and young adults.

This highly distinctive name, just like the name GREY-HOUND, worked to promote the business and to position it above its competition. A U.S. District Court found the name JELLI-BEANS, when used in connection with a skating rink, to be so strong that the court extended its sphere of monopoly to prevent the use of any other kind of candy-related words by competitors. When another skating rink tried to open in the same neighborhood under the name LOLLIPOPS, it was summarily enjoined from using that name. The newcomer appealed. In upholding the injunction, the circuit judges stated:

> There is a strong likelihood that roller skaters will confuse LOLLIPOPS with JELLIBEANS. . . . [JELLIBEANS] service mark is distinctive and is entitled to broad protection. . . .

This is a good example of the protection role fulfilled by a good commercial name, as was discussed in Chapter 2.

But there is more to the name JELLIBEANS. In addition to its high degree of distinctiveness and enforceability, the name has a remarkable aesthetic quality. The word JELLIBEANS flows harmoniously, thanks to the use of two liquid syllables and one labial syllable: JEL–LI–BEANS. The aural suggestion is that of the joyful sound of jingling bells. The accentuation of the first syllables gives the word enough impact to make it stand out in the flow of conversation. The creator of the name, however, may not have appreciated all its aesthetic qualities. It could be that he was subconsciously inspired to select that name. The fact remains that he has created an effective commercial designation perfectly tuned to his audience.

The name JELLIBEANS, in addition to being a successful use of a suggestive or symbolic term (like GREYHOUND), shows us that a distinctive name deserves a large aura of protection. This example also is proof that the syllables of a word can be effectively used to add aesthetic accents to a commercial name to help predispose the targeted audience toward the named enterprise, goods, or services.

NYQUIL

With the trademark NYQUIL for a nightime colds medicine, we are making a quantum jump from names borrowed from the English language, such as GREYHOUND and JELLIBEANS, toward coined names entirely fabricated for the occasion. The mark NYQUIL was adopted in the late 1960s by Richardson-Vicks, Inc. of Wilton, Connecticut, the manufacturer of the famous VICKS VAPORUB ointment. The NYQUIL name is remarkable because its message contents are very subtly carried by two word fragments—*Ny* for night and *quil* from tranquil—promising a quiet night to the poor coughing and sneezing customer. The message transcends the product itself and its qualities to define the benefits that the prospective buyer will derive from the purchase. This intimate involvement of the buyer in the name's commercial message denotes a very astute marketing acumen on the part of the product's promoter. One must also admire the manner in which the complex message is couched in a single, memorable two-syllable word. This type of commercial name goes one step further than GREYHOUND and JELLI-BEANS to convey a clear promise about the efficiency of the product. The fact that the name is made from whole cloth guarantees its uniqueness and legal clout.

KODAK

In 1888, George Eastman, a shrewd entrepreneur who could be called the "Henry Ford" of the photographic business, understood very well the importance of a distinctive name. While looking for a corporate identity and a trademark, he set the following criteria: a short word that meant nothing, that could not be easily misspelled, and that would have a strong aural impact. After trying various combinations of syllables, he settled on the name KODAK. That name has much to offer. The hard guttural and dental sounds give the word a forceful impact. The two *k*'s work like bookends to frame the word's compactness and emphasize its symmetry. KODAK established a fashion and was followed by a flock of other commercial identifiers beginning and/or ending with *k,* to wit: KLEENEX, KOTEX, POZ-I-LOK, MICRO-LOK, KOMPACK, and KAL-DEK. KODAK is so strong and so distinctive that after a century it remains the best name in its field. It has helped the Eastman Kodak Company to maintain a dominant position in the market.

With the name KODAK, we have gone one step further into the realms of the fanciful and the distinctive. Instead of using a word borrowed from the English language or combining meaningful word fragments (as in NYQUIL), KODAK was coined from meaningless syllables. In doing this, one forfeits the inherent impression that flows from the original meaning of a borrowed word and the semantic contents of word fragments. The impact or engram of the word upon the mind must depend entirely upon the combination of letters and sound, thereby rendering the task of creating an effective commercial name more difficult. However, the singularity of a coined word such as KODAK endows it with so much distinctiveness that its legal strength and effectiveness are unmatched.

HANG TEN

This series of exemplary commercial names ends with a more recent creation: the mark HANG TEN used in connection with the sale of polo-style shirts and other casual garments. HANG TEN was borrowed from the jargon of Southern California surfers. It refers to the act of keeping all of one's ten toes on the surfboard. When first used as a trademark, HANG TEN was only intelligible to a relatively limited class of adolescents. But this was the very class of customers to whom the product was directed. The response was immediate, and the mark, with its two-footprint logo, was an instant success.

The business was taken over by some very shrewd operators who became convinced that it would be more lucrative to have the garments made and sold through licensees in exchange for royalties than to handle it themselves. The company forsook any manufacturing activity to concentrate on the development and policing of a licensing program. First they operated in the United States; then, as the popularity of the mark expanded overseas, manufacturing and selling licenses were granted in England, France, West Germany, Japan, and finally, in seventy-four other countries throughout the world.

The mark HANG TEN took the place of a competitive product as the stock-in-trade of the business and became the business's most valuable asset. Such a metamorphosis of a commercial name from a simple indication of origin to an independently exploitable property is not an uncommon phenomenon. It can be planned and should be sought by any astute entrepreneur. The elevation of a good commercial name to becoming a lucrative source of revenues should be part of the business plan of any new company. The prerequisite is the creation of a strong and effective name.

In the mark HANG TEN are most of the desirable characteristics attributed earlier to GREYHOUND, JELLIBEANS,

NYQUIL, and KODAK, in particular its close affinity with the targeted class of buyers, its originality, and its aural impact.

From the preceding analysis, we can isolate the following key attributes of a good commercial name:

1. It must be on target; that is, it must be addressed to the intended class of consumers.
2. It must be motivating; that is, it must cause the customer to select the product or services offered by the firm.
3. It must be memorable; that is, it must stick in the consumer's mind.
4. It must be strong legally; that is, it must be distinctive.

CHAPTER 5

LEGAL FACTORS

Regardless of how motivating or memorable a term is, it will make a poor commercial name if it has no legal clout, such clout being the ability to prevent the adoption or imitation of that name by others.

DEGREES OF STRENGTH

Judges have defined a whole spectrum of potency for commercial names based on the name's degree of descriptiveness. At the top of the list, purely arbitrary names without any intrinsic meaning, like KODAK, are considered very strong legally and deserving of a broad scope of protection. At the bottom of that list are generic names, such as COMPUTER MERCHANT, that, being no more than a plain English definition of the type of activity or product they designate, cannot belong exclusively to anyone. Between those two extremes lies a variety of hues qualified as mildly suggestive, suggestive, highly suggestive, mildly descriptive, merely descriptive, and common descriptive terms.

The following examples are compiled from the rulings of various tribunals:

Generic Names (No Protection)

AIR-SHUTTLE (for back-and-forth air travel)

Commonly Descriptive Names (No Protection)

LITE (for low-calorie beer)
CONSUMER ELECTRONICS (for electronics magazine)

DIAL-A-RIDE (for bus service ordered by phone)

READER (for tabloid)

SURGICENTERS (for surgical care centers)

SAFARI (for safari-style outfits)

Merely Descriptive (Protected Once Well Established)

COMPUTERLAND (for computer store)

FISH-FRI and CHICK-FRI (for batter mixes)

PARROT JUNGLE (for tourist attraction featuring parrots)

TELEMED (for computer analysis of electrocardiograms by phone)

VISION CENTER (for optometric service center)

Highly Suggestive Names (Protectible)

CITIBANK (for banking services)

OLD HEARTH (for bakery goods)

UNDERNEATH IT ALL (for women's undergarments)

ULTRASUEDE (for suedelike fabric)

Suggestive Names (Protectible)

OILEX (for lubricants)

REJUVIA (for skin care product)

SLICKCRAFT (for recreational boat)

VISA (for financial services)

Fanciful Names (Protectible)

JELLIBEANS (for skating rink)

KODAK (for photographic products)

These characterizations are not totally consistent and reflect the confusing state of commercial name protection jurisprudence in the United States.

ENFORCEABILITY

The practical advantage of a legally strong commercial name is its easy enforceability, that is, the ability to prevent others from adopting the same or a similar name. This enforceability can be shown in two different areas: first, in the scope of the monopoly accorded to that name, both in terms of field of use and degree of similarity; and second, in the use of summary legal proceedings.

Scope of Monopoly

As demonstrated in the JELLIBEANS case in Chapter 4, the name JELLIBEANS was found to deserve a broad scope of monopoly in terms of the degree of similarity since the name LOLLIPOPS was ruled to be within that scope. To state as the court did in this case that the terms JELLIBEANS and LOLLIPOPS are similar might seem rather odd. But given the circumstances of the case and in consideration of the broad scope of monopoly recognized to JELLIBEANS, that statement makes sense.

The court in that case did not have to define the extent of the applicable field of use since the defendant was operating a skating rink, just like the plaintiff. It has already been mentioned that GREYHOUND CORPORATION was able to prevent the application of the name GREYHOUND to an unrelated financial service. In another case, resulting from the appropriation of the very strong name HALLMARK, the court ruled that, although the plaintiff used the mark only in connection with the sale of greeting cards, the preempted field of use extended to the defendant's automobile dealership.

In fact, the preempted field of use to which a very distinctive mark is entitled may be limitless. The name KODAK, for instance, could not be used by anyone without a license from the Eastman Kodak Company, regardless of the type of goods or services contemplated. Indeed, the name is so well known that the public would immediately attribute sponsorship of these products or services to the famous photographic equipment manufacturer. This perceived sponsorship or source of origin, if not true, would be deceptive and could not be tolerated.

Summary Proceedings

The JELLIBEANS story also illustrates how easily a distinctive commercial name can be protected without recourse to protracted and costly legal procedures. The appeal was taken from a preliminary injunction issued by the district court, pending trial on the issue.

A lawsuit usually begins with the parties filing their pleadings—complaint, answer with or without cross-complaint, demurrers, motions to strike or to dismiss, and so on—until all the factual and legal issues have been clearly put before the court. This is followed by a period of discovery, during which each contestant is allowed to look into its opponent's case by way of interrogatories and requests for admissions, depositions of parties and witnesses, requests for production of documentary evidence, and so on. Finally, when both parties are ready, the case is brought to trial before a judge or a jury. Further delay may be incurred to hear motions to resolve procedural questions before trial. The process goes on for months and often years, during which time lawyers are very busy building up their cases and billing their clients accordingly.

However, when certain issues of fact or law are incontestably established, summary legal proceedings are sometimes available to obtain a quick and often final judgment or a temporary but binding order pending trial. The legal strength of an allegedly infringed commercial name is often the most important issue to be resolved in a name misappropriation case. If that strength is inherent to the name due to the name's highly distinctive character, an ex parte restraining order or a preliminary injunction may be readily obtained by the plaintiff. An ex parte order is an extraordinary remedy granted without giving the defendant an opportunity to present his case before the court. Its purpose is to avoid or limit irreparable damages. The disparagement of a commercial name has been ruled to be an irreparable injury that can justify the extraordinary remedy of an ex parte order forbidding the defendant from using the name. Certain statutes even provide for ex parte orders to seize and confiscate goods bearing a counterfeit mark before they enter the flow of commerce. If the circumstances do not warrant the issue of an ex parte order, the plaintiff nevertheless may obtain the same type of remedy through a preliminary injunction following a special hearing with both parties present but on short notice, provided that the plaintiff can demonstrate a good probability of winning the trial.

Finally, if all the issues relating to the infringement are well settled, the court can issue a summary judgment that can be a final adjudication of the claim. While such a judgment is always desirable, an ex parte order or a preliminary injunction may be as effective in disposing of the case. Once a defendant has been enjoined from using the disputed name, the plaintiff has no incentive to bring the case to an early trial. The defendant, for his part, must adopt another name to stay in business and after a while has no reason to return to his first but presently forbidden choice. He will most likely abandon the litigation or seek a quick settlement with the plaintiff.

Accordingly, the rule of the game in name infringement actions is to obtain enforcement of one's exclusive rights by way of summary proceedings. Once a restraining order or injunction has been issued, there is only a remote chance that the case will be taken to trial because the defendant will in most cases give up the fight after having been temporarily prevented from using the disputed name.

In the opposite case, where the plaintiff fails to obtain relief in a preliminary action due to the weakness of the allegedly infringed name, he often will switch to a more defensible trademark or trade name rather than put up with the confusion created by the adoption of his original name by the defendant. In either case, there is little incentive on anyone's part to pursue the litigation. The creation of a highly distinctive name will assure success in summary proceedings, but the selection of a descriptive name will only enmesh the name's owner in futile and costly litigations.

Those fortunate enough to have avoided protracted law proceedings may think that resorting to a lawsuit would be quicker and easier than the quest for a good name. In some cases, that just might be true, but if the legalities should turn sour, Hamlet's distress at having to bear "the proud man's contumely, the pangs of disprized love, the law's delay" would have to be suffered all over again.

HIGH WIRE ACT

A legally strong commercial name carries enough clout to assure a quick and inexpensive prevention of its appropriation. It is therefore imperative that a mark or trade name be selected or created with a good understanding of all the factors that a court would take into consideration in assessing the name's legal strength in the event of an infringement action.

We already know that fanciful names, such as KODAK and JELLIBEANS, which have no direct relation to the business or goods they identify, are inherently very strong. We also have been warned that generic or commonly descriptive terms, such as SUPER GLUE and LITE, can never be monopolized. But what about all the names that range from merely descriptive to highly suggestive? How does a court gauge their legal strength? After all, a somewhat descriptive term might be preferable in some cases.

The general rule is that the legal strength of a commercial name is inversely proportional to its degree of descriptive relationship to the named product or the activities of the named concern. However, the court will also take into account the standing of the name in the public mind as a result of long and exclusive use by the original owner, extensive advertising, and commercial success. These factors are said to confer on a descriptive name a **secondary meaning** in the public mind, whereby a descriptive name such as INTERNATIONAL BUSINESS MACHINES no longer designates any manufacturer of business equipment but clearly identifies the giant and ubiquitous IBM.

Thus, a somewhat descriptive commercial name can achieve a certain degree of distinction and at the same time acquire a great deal of legal strength through secondary meaning. However, deliberately selecting a descriptive name and counting on the rapid acquisition of secondary meaning to boost the name's legal clout is a very risky high wire act. Some courts have ruled that secondary meaning can only be tacked to a descriptive name through long and exclusive use. In other words, if the same name is used by another during the early period, when no infringement is possible, the name will never acquire secondary meaning because it designates more than a single source of goods or services. Furthermore, secondary meaning is not usually taken for granted by courts and must be supported by factual evidence, something that cannot practically be done in the confined circumstances of a preliminary legal procedure. The person trying to enforce an exclusive claim to a descriptive term on the basis of secondary meaning may have to wait until trial to prove his case. We know what an intolerable and frustrating situation this may create for the plaintiff. Finally, since a descriptive name is part of the common language, it can never be completely monopolized. The law provides that, no matter how strong a descriptive name and how much secondary meaning has attached to it, its owner cannot prevent its **fair use** by those who employ it to describe their own goods or the activities of their own firm. The concluding recommendation is that descriptive terms be used sparingly in creating commercial names. This recommendation applies only in those circumstances when extensive publicity and other mass marketing methods are available to develop a great deal of secondary meaning in a very short period of time and when the risk of loss is acceptable. Small entrepreneurs and companies with limited resources should avoid descriptive terms like the plague.

You should now have a good appreciation for the attributes of a strong and successful commercial name. It is important to understand that an almost perfect coincidence exists between the legal requirements and the market-oriented criteria that govern the selection of a strong and effective name. They can be expressed in a single word—distinctiveness. The remaining chapters are devoted to the means and methods of creating legally strong and at the same time commercially effective names.

PART 2

THE METHOD

I can interweave such genteel words. . . .
—*Troubadour Peire Vidal (1180–1205)*

CHAPTER 6

OUTLINE

The method that is about to be defined for creating commercial names is only one of many possible approaches to a sometimes difficult and frustrating task. Yet, it is a method that has consistently yielded very strong and effective names. It is presented here as a direct application of the rules and principles discussed in the preceding chapters.

The complete process of name creation is illustrated in Figure 6–1 and can be divided into two basic phases. Phase 1 consists of defining the message to be conveyed. Phase 2 covers the translation of that message into a commercial name in compliance with all the principles discussed earlier. Many of the steps within each phase of the process would benefit from the contributions of expert professionals in the fields of marketing, semantics, psychology, and the law. While those contributions are necessary to do a truly professional job, an enterprising individual with a good understanding of the rules should be able to create a valuable commercial name with minimum outside help by following step-by-step the suggested method, with the caveat that the availability and the enforceability of the name should be confirmed by a competent trademark lawyer.

OVERVIEW

Phase 1 begins with a crucial fact-gathering process in the form of a comprehensive inquiry about the market in which the new commercial name is to be used and about the nature of the services or products that will be offered under that name. Con-

FIGURE 6–1
The Process of Commercial Name Creation.

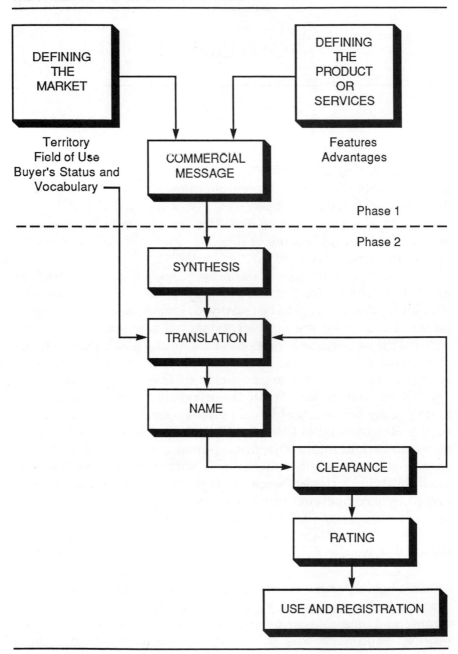

trary to what you might presume, the information relative to the market is far more important to the naming process than the type and attributes of the product. Some of the exemplary names, such as JELLIBEANS and HANG TEN, discussed in Chapter 4, were created to fit the prospective customer, with no particular relationship to the goods or services the names represent. It is indeed possible to create a very effective name, based on a good acquaintance with the market, without knowing anything about the product. The opposite is impossible.

The bulk of the data collected during the fact-finding process are used to formulate the commercial message that should be conveyed by the name. Information about the vocabulary of the prospective customers or buyers will control the translation of that message into the desired name.

The formulation of the commercial message, as you will soon appreciate, is the most fascinating aspect of the whole semonemic process because it calls for the contributions of other creative individuals. The recommended step of actually devising a form of television commercial offers some great opportunities for rallying all interested parties in support of the name-maker's endeavor.

Phase 2 is initiated by a task almost as tedious as the fact-gathering process—the synthesis of the commercial message into a simple theme or image that carries the essence of that message. The fun returns with the translation of that theme or image into a few simple words or phrases that constitute the prospective name candidates. It is in the translation process that the name-smith can exercise his linguistic and poetic talents.

The clearance of the name is a legal process that necessitates the initial retention of a trade name and trademark practitioner. It raises several complex issues that you must learn to distinguish if you want your name to survive the treacherous legal minefield of the marketplace. If none of the candidate names passes legal muster, you must return to the translation process to create new ones. If it appears that you have exhausted all possibilities of rendering the synthesized commercial message, you may have to return to phase 1 to formulate a new one.

Once you have succeeded in clearing two or more good name prospects, the rating method outlined in Chapter 14 will help you in selecting the most effective one. Proper use and registration are discussed in Chapter 15 for the benefit of the lucky beneficiary of your creative talents.

START WITH A CLEAN SLATE

The prescribed method is based on the assumption that the name-maker is undertaking his task without any personal preconceived idea about what the name to be created should be like, and without having any criteria imposed upon him by his employer's or client's management or marketing department, or by any other party. This assumption is necessary to assure the most objective approach to the name creation.

Such an ideal condition is rare. It is extremely difficult to rid oneself completely of preconceived ideas and to convince an employer or client that he should give you complete freedom of action. In fact, the employer or client should at some time have an opportunity to contribute to the name-fabrication process. The method does provide, in the initial fact-gathering phase, for the collecting of information from various sources, the foremost of which being the business's owner or manager. Marketing people should also actively participate when formulating the message to be conveyed by the name. That is to say, no confining parameter should be imposed upon the name-maker at the outset. Outsiders' contributions should be brought into the name-minting process in due time and for the exact purpose specified by the method, not as mandatory provisions that could distort the course of events that are aiming to produce the most appropriate name for the occasion.

An insistence on the part of the marketing department that the new corporate identifier should, for instance, include the term *general* to reflect the diversified activities of the company would be a regrettable usurpation of the name-maker's prerogatives. This would unduly limit the list of semonemic methods normally available for coining the name. Instead, the marketing request should be entered as a well-articulated commercial during the message-definition phase. The choice of words in the translation of that message is best left to the expertise of the semonemician. Along the same line, a requirement by a cosmetics manufacturer that the name of a new product be a French word, based on the manufacturer's belief that his female customers respond more favorably to Gallic terms than to English ones, could be self-defeating. It would force the name-maker to bypass several of the most creative steps of the coining process and to miss the opportunity to mint the most effective brand name in French, Italian, or any other appropriate language.

A few tips are now offered as to how to start on the right foot with the cooperative understanding and support of all interested parties.

DEALING WITH THE AD-MAN

In many organizations, the creation of a commercial name—whether a new corporate identifier or a brand for a new product or service—is seen, and justifiably so, as a marketing task. Chapter 2 already spotlighted the promotional value of commercial names. A name is a promise, that is, an advertisement. Responsibility for its creation and management lies primarily with the marketing department, but advertising people are not necessarily experts at coining commercial identifiers. While the ad-man is responsible for the preparation of promotional brochures and radio advertisements, he is not necessarily a skilled photographer, a talented jingle composer, or an astute commercial name-maker. Photography, the composition of jingles, and semonemics are separate disciplines that demand special talents not necessarily found in a marketing expert. Linguistic proficiency and legal acumen are required for a skilled namesmith and may not be part of the ad-man's stock-in-trade. The name-maker, however, needs information and guidance from the marketing personnel in defining the marketplace for the name-to-be. Furthermore, as stated earlier, the formulation of the commercial message to be conveyed through the name can benefit from the active participation of the advertising expert. Therefore, in dealing with the ad-man, the semonemician must attempt to carefully delineate the roles of the contributing parties to ensure their productive cooperation and avoid any disruptive interference. For the ad-man even to suggest to the name-maker any type of brand name for a new product would indeed constitute a damaging interference with the name-coining process, like humming a few bars to a musician hired to compose a jingle. The ad-man's input must come in good time and in good order, and be apropos, as will be indicated in the following chapters.

DEALING WITH THE B.O.D.

Helping the advertising people to understand their proper role in the name-creating process should be relatively easy since they themselves often endure in their creative endeavors the annoying dictates of other services, or of the management, on matters that should rightfully be left to the advertising department. Dealing with the board of directors or the owners and top management of a firm, on the other hand, can be quite a challenge for the diplomatic savoir faire of the name-maker. Directors may not be linguistic or marketing professionals, yet they may be perfectly convinced in their own minds that they can make a valuable contribution to the name-creating process.

It is frequently a major task to convince the B.O.D. that commercial names cannot be selected or created by committees. As was mentioned in the Preface in connection with the Oklahoma Osteopathic Hospital case, disastrous results can be expected from the selection of a name by a panel of interested, but not necessarily enlightened, individuals. Persuading the directors that the job can be better accomplished with the help of an outside consultant requires a great deal of salesmanship and diplomatic skill.

Owners and top executives may also attempt to impose rigid guidelines upon the name-makers. For instance, in a quest for a new corporate identity, the management may insist upon some degree of continuity between the old and new names. The Preface already reported Consolidated Foods' vain efforts to find an acceptable variation of that name. Under similar constraints, some recent name changes have been achieved by contracting, collapsing, or abbreviating old identifiers, with no gain in semantic value or memorability.

It is therefore imperative that you, as a name-maker, insist upon obtaining carte blanche from management to forge the most effective name possible, using every type of arrow from your semonemic quiver. You should keep your employer's staff informed of your progress to lay the groundwork for the disclosure of your final creation. Due to their preconceived ideas, these executives may expect a name totally different from the one you will eventually deliver to them. If they are not properly primed and educated along the way, you may find it difficult to sell them the fruits of your labor in a single, final, quantum step.

CHAPTER 7

GATHERING THE FACTS

In Chapter 1, we discussed the function of names as goodwill ambassadors and heralds. The role of an ambassador or a herald is to deliver a message. Accordingly, the first step in creating a name is to define the message that must be delivered to the prospective customer. That message may be some exalting information about the named firm or product or a motivating thought that must be implanted into the mind of the customer. That message, however, cannot be formulated until all the pertinent facts relative to the thing to be named have been gathered.

DEFINING THE MARKET

Whether a firm is in business to manufacture goods, such as furniture, or to deliver services, such as real estate brokerage, these goods or services are intended for a particular marketplace. That marketplace can be defined in terms of territory, field of use, and type of customer.

Territory

If the territory includes foreign countries, the created name needs to be compatible with the languages and cultural backgrounds of the various nationalities populating those countries. Even the domestic market is not uniform, and the name-maker should know whether the territory covers the entire nation, as is the case for most packaged goods, or whether the goods or services are addressed to a local market. There are enough ethnic, climatic, and living style differences in the United States to warrant different choices of commercial names.

Field of Use

The field of use—that is, whether we are dealing with a household product or a professional tool, and whether the service is to be offered in the home, on the street, or in a business environment—needs to be clearly defined. For instance, a drug that must be prescribed by a physician will not be the subject of a mass advertising campaign but will be marketed via personal sales calls, erudite articles in professional publications, and seminars. By contrast, an over-the-counter remedy for the common cold will need mass advertising in popular magazines and on television. Since the message for each of these drugs must be delivered in very different ways, each message must be couched in the form most appropriate to the mode of delivery. Whereas the former may safely be sold under a complex brand name of appreciable length, the name to be used in mass advertising of the latter must necessarily be short and incisive and have a strong aural impact. ERCEFURYL and ACETAMINOPHEN may constitute adequate names for prescription medicines but would not lend themselves to television advertising in the way that such marks as CONTAC and ADVIL do.

The Customer

Knowing where and under what circumstances the product will be used or the services will be rendered helps in drawing the profile of the typical buyer or customer. To continue with our drug examples, the person to whom the prescription drug must be sold is primarily the physician, whereas the over-the-counter common cold remedy is most likely to be purchased with the weekly groceries by the typical homemaker. These two types of customers exhibit significant differences in their educations, social and economical status, tastes, aspirations, and common vocabulary.

It would be futile to couch a message in true King's English if the recipient comprehends only Spanish or ghetto vernacular.

Due to differences in their education and milieu, a physician perceives a name in a different manner from a farmhand. It is therefore necessary to analyze the audience before writing the speech.

Social and Educational Status
An individual's level of education, social status, and profession in most cases determines his aspirations and motivation. An upper-level corporate management executive is manifestly more interested in acquiring broader powers in the corporate structure and more prestige in his community than more money. He is most likely responsive to such commercial names as DIPLOMAT or POWERBUILT. A young aspiring executive whose main goal is to climb the corporate ladder is probably more responsive to such names as STRIDE, MERIT, or PROMO. The middle-aged blue-collor worker who has reached a plateau in personal advancement may be motivated by the prospect of pleasant recreational activities on weekends and during vacation from work. Words like CRUISE or RIVIERA are more likely to catch this individual's attention.

Vocabulary
The level of education and social status of the customer dictate the vocabulary from which the most effective commercial name may be drawn. Various classes of vocabularies and their typical levels of corresponding social stratification follow.

Scholastic	Physicians, scientists, and members of academia
King's English	Corporate executives, professionals, and other college graduates
Common English	Small business owners, blue-collar workers, and high-school students
Puerile	Children, recent immigrants, and nonassimilated minorities

The scholastic vocabulary includes learned words made from classical Greek and Latin roots, such as *praxis* and *modulus,* and most of the scientific nomenclature. Names of prescription medicines, such as METHOCARBAMOL and ERYTHROMYCIN, are often drawn from this vocabulary.

King's English includes all the correct dictionary-sanctioned terms of the language and archaic forms. Such marks as THISTLE and ARPEGGIO are derived from this class of words.

Common English can be said to be limited to the spoken vocabulary of the artisan, blue-collar, and other middle classes. It incorporates most colloquialisms. JELLIBEANS, AIM, PAPERMATE, and CHUCK WAGON are good examples of names made from common English words.

The puerile vocabulary is restricted to the most basic terms of the language first learned by toddlers. It is the base for such marks as MR BUBBLE, MR CLEAN, and TWINKIES. The Young Adult Literacy Assessment Report published by the U.S. Department of Education in September, 1986 reveals that 5 percent of people ages twenty-one to twenty-five read below the fourth-grade level and another 15 percent read below the eighth-grade level. These statistics indicate that as many as fifty million adult residents of the United States may not be able to comprehend words above this puerile classification. Such widespread illiteracy requires that all commercial names for consumer goods be drawn from the lower classifications.

More than one vocabulary class may be suitable for the intended audience. The secret is to remain within the chosen classification when translating the message into a company name or a mark. Let us examine, for example, the term FOCUS. This term has been adopted by dozens of enterprises for various forms of commercial names, from a trademark for jewelry to a real estate broker's trade name, and lately to identify a chain of department stores. The erudite word has been borrowed in extenso from Latin and may be placed on the borderline between the King's English and common English. Its meaning is probably beyond the grasp of a large segment of the population. Consequently, its use should be limited to the designation of products and services addressed to the more highly educated individual, unless one is to rely on its general *impression* rather than its actual *meaning* to carry the intended commercial message. What type of impression can the term FOCUS be expected to create upon the mind of an unsophisticated customer unfamiliar with its significance? Is it going to be in the sense of a center of attraction, concentration, or attention to detail that a literate person would perceive in that name? Unfortunately not. There is nothing in the sound of the word FOCUS that could connote that kind of meaning. There is, in fact, a good chance that the term will plainly or subconsciously evoke the verboten acronym. The scatological connotation is further reinforced by the sound of the final syllable, which is homonymous to the word *cuss*. Spanish, French, and other Romance language speakers may even hear in that last syllable another scurrilous word evolved from the Latin *culus*. Using a learned word to designate a product or service can have unpredictable consequences if it is addressed to an unsophisticated audience. It is impossible to always anticipate the kind of association that such a word will bring to the mind of individuals who do not readily sense its true meaning. When UAL, Inc., the parent of United Airlines, adopted the name ALLEGIS, a company spokesperson proudly announced that the new corporate identifier was derived from the words *allegiant* (meaning loyal) and *aegis* (meaning shield or protector). These two words belong to the upper reaches of the King's English and could only be discerned, not to mention understood, by a relatively small number of learned individuals. To most people, ALLEGIS simply reminds of allergies.

One could also make the opposite error by selecting an ordinary word, or coining an apparently simple one, addressed to the common individual just for its pleasant phonetic character. Unless one takes into account the learned meaning of that word or the impression it may create upon a more sophisticated audience, the results might be quite surprising or even ludicrous. For example, there is a long list of Japanese automobiles with feminine names ending with the letter *a*, notably ACURA, INTEGRA, and CRESSIDA. Those names were undoubtedly selected for their high phonetic impact, but they also have meanings, at least for certain people. The Latin roots of ACURA imply sharpness, precision, and accuracy. Their relationship to an automobile must concern the precision applied to the car's fabrication. Is that the technical claim that the manufacturer intended to convey through the name ACURA? The message is a bit muddled. INTEGRA suggests integrity to most people. What the integrity of a vehicle might be, again, is subject to some conjecture. But INTEGRA can also mean whole, unspoiled, and, in the feminine form of that name, virginal, as in the Marian hymn: "Inviolata, integra et casta" (Thou art untouched, virginal, and chaste)! CRESSIDA, by contrast, is the name of the legendary fickle Trojan dame in the works of Chaucer and Shake-speare. Thus, while some of our contemporaries drive down the freeways proclaiming their virginity with the name INTEGRA etched in silver letters on their cars, others unashamedly publicize their infidelity under the CRESSIDA vocable. (All Toyota dealers will assure you that CRESSIDA implies no reflection upon the car's reliability.)

DEFINING THE PRODUCT OR SERVICES

Having defined the audience, we must now look at the product or the service to articulate the message that the commercial name must convey to the customer. Indeed, it is necessary to understand fully the nature, characteristics, functions, and main advantages of the thing to be named before we can say something positive about it. In doing so, we must focus on the particular attributes and beneficial effects that distinguish this product or service from those offered by the competition. This requires a good knowledge of the market, acquired if possible by interviewing the sales and marketing personnel. All pertinent information must be duly noted and considered, although only the quintessence of all the data gathered may eventually be translated into the final name. It is extremely important to assemble the most complete set of information before attempting to coin the name. Listing all findings in order of importance facilitates the translation task when unavoidable critical choices must be made, as between features or advantages that will be reflected in the final version of the name.

When the task entails the naming of a company, the analysis must be focused upon the services the company renders to the public, rather than upon the nature, size, and internal structure of the business. What must be emphasized are the characteristics of these services that are particularly attractive to the customer. The fact that a particular life insurance company has the largest actuarial data base in the nation is of little concern to most prospective subscribers. These individuals, however, would be very interested if they were told that the company has consistently paid the highest dividends among all life insurance companies during the last ten years.

When seeking a name for a product, you should emphasize the most interesting aspect of the product from the user's point of view, as opposed to the design engineer's. The buyer is not going to be much influenced by the fact that a vacuum cleaner was assembled on a line using the latest advances in production robotics but may be far more impressed by the power and quietness of the vacuum cleaner's new motor.

Engineers are not the only ones to blame for aiming off target. Salespeople love to promote the features of a new product because that is what they spend most of their time selling. They sometimes fail to realize that buyers care more about the benefits they can derive from those features than about the actual features themselves. The quietness of the vacuum cleaner must be related to the perspective of the user; it must be translated into advantageous results closely impinging upon the user's daily life. For example, the salesperson should point out that the running of the vacuum cleaner will not disturb the baby's sleep or the tranquility of the downstairs neighbors.

PRODUCT LIFE

The last market-oriented characteristic of the product or service is the time span during which the name is expected to be in use. A product line that has an expected market life of only a few years can be offered under a mark derived from a contemporary, even faddish, and somewhat ephemeral term. How many of today's teenagers would know about the PET ROCK? By contrast, corporate names and brands for staple goods call for more enduring terms.

EXAMPLES

It would be difficult to elaborate on this subject without reference to some concrete examples. Some cases have been selected from the files of Alias, the commercial name laboratory service operating in San Diego, California. (We will continue to cite examples from the Alias case files throughout the remainder of this book.)

In one case, the client needed a brand name for a new type of candy. More specifically, the goods consisted of a form of peanut-butter confection shaped like a chocolate-chip cookie wrapped in foil. The client referred to it as a type of marzipan. Upon further inquiry, it was discovered that the goods were an imitation of a sweet very popular in Mexico. They were intended for sale on the domestic market to Mexican-Americans and also

in Mexico. The typical buyers were further defined as adult immigrants from Mexico, to whom the confection would bring pleasant and nostalgic reminiscences of the type of candy they used to buy as children in their mother country. Given this consumer profile, it was decided that the name had to be derived not only from Spanish but from a typically Mexican term and that it must exhibit a childlike simplicity. What was needed was a short Mexican word that would be mellifluous and easy to pronounce.

The semonemical process in this particular case yielded the mark CHAPULIN. This word of Aztec origin means locust, cicada, or grasshopper. This insect symbol appears often in the pre-Columbian frescoes and hieroglyphs of Mexico. Chapultepec, which means "the hill of the locusts," was the last stronghold defended by Cuauhtemoc against the conquistadores. The word

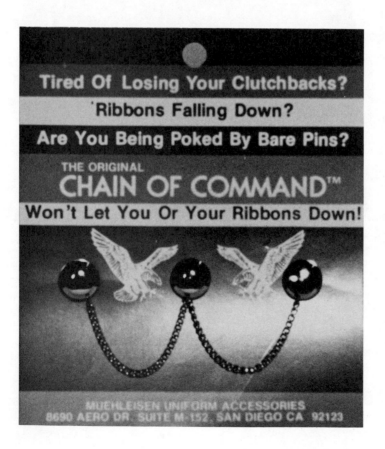

CHAPULIN has therefore a strong association within the targeted market with Mexican history and patriotism. The same word is also used in Mexico as a term of endearment for a child. CHAPULIN thus carries the other element of the desired message, which is childhood nostalgia. This particular choice of commercial name, with its sharply focused class of targeted customer, is a good example of identification between the product name and the buyer and illustrates how critical it is to clearly define the market before selecting the name of the product.

In another case, the product was a device sold in uniform shops to military personnel for securing multiple rows of ribbon decorations onto a breast pocket. The device resembled a series of tiepins with clip-backs, joined together by small chains. The targeted audience was easily defined as upper-echelon, career military personnel. Without entering into the other aspects of the message contents of the name, let us simply state that the final choice was CHAIN OF COMMAND. This is a term that is constantly used in military life and therefore one with which the intended customer could not fail to identify. Through the bias of a play on the word CHAIN, a strong link was established in the customer's mind between the goods and his career. The result was a highly memorable, distinctive, and effective brand name, perfectly tailored to the market.

CHAPTER 8

THE MESSAGE

The examples discussed in Chapter 7 present a glimpse of the message contents of some commercial names. Defining that message is a crucial step in the naming process and may require the help of a marketing expert.

SORTING THE PROMOTIONAL FACTORS

From the mass of information gathered during the fact-finding exercise, only the determinative factors—that is, those factors that truly influence buyer preference—should be retained. This will help to direct the name toward the area where it will be most effective in promoting the product or service. Obviously, only a limited number of features can be considered for inclusion in the message, but care must be taken not to overlook the most motivating ones. Prior market studies about the product or company should be analyzed. If no prior marketing research results are available, a survey designed to elicit the most determinative features of the product or company may be indicated.

In preparing this type of survey, you should not confuse the perceived importance of a feature with its relevance to the customer's choice. For instance, all surveyed individuals may emphatically state that it is important that a toothpaste contain cavity-inhibiting fluoride. However, further inquiry may reveal that their choice among various brands is more often influenced by the flavor of the toothpaste than by its composition. Only those characteristics that are relevant to the consumer's choice should be considered. This process should allow the sifting out of a great deal of insignificant data, while lending more objectivity to the formulation of the promotional message.

The general tenor of the message will begin to emerge as the most determinant features are elicited. A buyer determinance survey for vacuum cleaners may rank quietness and being lightweight far ahead of brand identification. In such a case, these two qualities should be the gist of the message to be carried by the name. If the product in question is a staple, such as flour or rice, the survey may show that the homemaker reacts mainly to the label or the design of the package. The message should then be aimed at catching the buyer's attention by focusing on the targeted customer's profile, as was done in the coining of the name CHAPULIN.

THE COMMERCIAL

Articulating the message is analogous to formulating a commercial. Having in mind all of the information gathered during the market and product definition phases, one should attempt as an exercise to write a motivating television commercial that will emphasize the most choice-determinating features identified during the survey. This commercial must use a totally bland and neutral designation for the goods or company, such as Brand X or XYZ Company. The task of formulating the commercials should be assigned, if possible, to several creative individuals working independently and separately from one another. A meeting may later be called to rate and compare the various commercials and to select the best, or to combine the contents of the top candidates into an optimally effective one. This process, if it is conducted according to the rules and principles of effective radio and television advertising, will bring to the surface those sounds and images that best promote the product or company.

The commercial so prepared will probably never be aired or even used except in the process of name selection. Nevertheless, this interim exercise must be conducted with all the care and expertise available because it is the key to the eventual creation of a truly effective commercial name. It is important to keep in mind throughout this process that a good commercial does not necessarily describe a product or service. It may not be objective or even rational. Many commercials rely on emotion or humor; so do effective names.

ADVERTISING FUNDAMENTALS

Television commercials and other advertising forms generally combine three ingredients: information, personal involvement, and emphasis.

Information may be about some unique feature or praise-worthy quality of the advertised product, such as the presence of vitamin E, a known emollient, in a skin lotion or the suitability of a new line of crockery for microwave cooking. The information may also relate to some newsworthy development, such as the endorsement of a new type of jogging shoes by the American Podiatrist Association.

Personal involvement is that part of the advertisement that attracts the attention of the consumer by responding to his taste or to one of his needs or cravings, or that calls for a judgment on his part about the desirability or appropriateness of the product. Using a term borrowed from surfers' lingo, as was done with HANG TEN, is bound to establish kinship with beach-goers. Showing some spots on the upholstery of a couch and demonstrating how easily and effectively a particular brand of cleaning foam removes them is a sure way to attract the attention of the housekeeper who happens to have a soiled davenport. In a way, personal involvement in a commercial fulfills the role of the salesperson who goes door-to-door peddling his wares. It puts the consumer in contact with the product. Effective use of this element always requires a thorough knowledge of the audience.

The last component is the brainwashing and sometimes irrational emphasis on one aspect of the product by means of high-impact sounds or images or by sheer repetitions. Such emphasis is the basic ingredient of commercial jingles and billboard advertising. As opposed to the other two components, which seek to interest the mind of the viewer or listener, emphasis is primarily addressed to the consumer's senses.

The dosage of each of these three elements in a commercial varies according to the nature of the item advertised. Unique and highly innovative products, such as a new type of contact lens, can be promoted with highly informative statements. Staple goods, such as laundry detergents, require a great deal of emphasis. The promotion of both types of products can benefit from a dose of personal involvement.

Given the limited confines of any commercial name and the legal objections to descriptive words, the commercial most favorable to the coining of that name is the one that uses a strong dose of emphasis with a relatively low level of information. Besides, the informative role of a commercial is necessarily limited. Persuasion is not the ultimate goal of most advertisers; they only want to capture the attention of their audience and maintain a certain degree of awareness of the object being promoted. With respect to commercial names, it is necessary only to create a name with enough impact and visibility to catch the attention of the targeted customer and to anchor itself permanently to the recesses of his memory.

For exercise and as a good example, let us return to the name LITE, which turned out to be so problematic for the Miller Brewing Company. Although the name choice was not well inspired, the commercials that introduced the new type of low-calorie brew to the American public were, by contrast, well presented, entertaining, and very effective. The commercials used a combination of "slice-of-life" scenes with the participation and testimonials of various celebrities from the sporting world. They combined some personal involvement with a great deal of emphasis. The general theme running through the commercials was that LITE was the choice of macho sport champions. The potential names that could have been derived from the theme are MACHO and CHAMP. Those names are not particularly brilliant by any standard, but they stand well above the commonly descriptive word LITE in terms of impact, memorability, and protection.

The major contribution that a marketing or public relations firm can bring to the semonemic process is the definition of the message that the name must convey to the customer. According to David Ogilvy, marketing people are not very successful at finding names acceptable to their clients, probably because they don't know the rules for creating commercial names or even that such rules exist. Their role, as we have defined here, can, however, be crucial in the professionally conducted naming of a firm and its products or services.

THE SYNTHESIS

Once you have

- analyzed the company, product, or services that are to be named,
- explored all the facets of the market,
- drawn a complete profile of the targeted customer, and
- composed a motivating radio or television commercial,

you hold all the elements necessary to create a truly pleasant and effective name to be used as a corporate identifier, trademark, or service mark. All that remains is to synthesize all the data, extract their quintessence, and translate it into a word or phrase. At first sight, this may appear to be the most difficult task, but it is a very exciting one that can be performed quite easily if the preliminary steps have been carefully conducted. Synthesizing the accumulated data calls for a certain amount of creativity, good communication skills, and competent legal advice. The most difficult step is to reduce the message contents of the commercial to a single theme, concept, or design that can be later conveyed with a single word or short phrase.

Every radio or television commercial carries a unifying theme—a leitmotiv that underscores the message or offers a particular scene that dramatizes the most important aspect of the article promoted. A serious situation arises, however, if there is no direct relationship between the name of the product and the memorable scene. The audience may remember the scene but will quickly forget the name of the product. To prove that point, here are some memorable lines and some striking sights from some quite familiar television commercials:

- "I can't believe I ate the whole thing!"
- "That's what I call a spicy meatball!"
- "Where's the beef?"
- "Why don't you pick one up and smoke it sometimes?"
- A washing machine that grows ten feet tall after the detergent is poured in
- A finicky cat by the name of Morris turning up his nose at some cat food
- A white tornado coming out of a kitchen
- A wild bull bursting through the wall of a bar

If you can ascribe a brand name to half of those sequences that you can remember, you have an excellent memory. To most people, the first quotation conjures indigestion, while the "spicy meatball" line conjures spicy meatballs. The beef inquiry reminds us of hamburgers, and Eddie Adam's invitation to a smoke reminds us of cigars. The hyperactive washer evokes a detergent. As for Morris, we remember that he does not like a certain type of cat food. The tornado has something to do with a cleanser. The crashing bull is promoting some alcoholic brew. In other words, these famous commercials are generic and could apply to any brand of similar products. They fall short of their goal, simply because the punch line is not in tune with the name of the product.

By contrast, anyone who remembers the white dove flying out of a bottle of dishwashing liquid or the miniature horse-drawn covered wagon scurrying through the kitchen while being chased by a dog has no trouble recalling the brand names DOVE and CHUCK WAGON. If you think that those sights are too specific, have you forgotten the brand name of the product advertised by showing huge crowns appearing suddenly on the heads of sandwich eaters? Can you conceive of a more effective way to engrave the name IMPERIAL in the psyche of the viewers?

The results of a survey on the impact of a series of full-page, four-color advertising appearing in forty-seven major magazines indicated that 44 percent noticed a particular ad and 35 percent could identify the brand name, but only 9 percent had read the contents. The point is that most of the commercial message in an advertisement will be lost if it is not carried by the name. In other words, the highlight of the commercial message must coincide with the name of the product. The converse is equally true. The name must reflect the high point of the most motivating commercial that can be devised. There is no chicken-or-egg dilemma in this equation. As we learned earlier, the name must promote the business or its product. The best way to promote something is by broadcasting an effective commercial. If the name is to fulfill a promotional role, a commercial must be first devised and the name derived from the commercial.

Here are two examples of commercial message synthesis taken from the Alias case file:

In the first instance, the product to be named was a tin cup with a folding handle especially designed for backpackers. The envisioned commercial showed a young man in shorts and hiking shoes, bending under a high-piled backpack to fill his XYZ cup from a waterfall. After draining the cup, the young man shakes it dry by tapping it none too lightly against a rock. The main theme relating to the potential user was "outdoors, active young adult." The salient feature of the product was its lightness and its rugged quality. The dominant element of the scene was the cascading water, the sound of which was echoed by the pinging tone of the cup hitting the rock. From that striking image, it was an easy step to name the product CASCADE. That word has everything that had to be conveyed—the sonorous solidity of the tin cup, as well as the feeling of wilderness with which the prospective buyers could identify. The name CASCADE is also effectively used in connection with a detergent for automatic dishwashers but lacks the measure of personal involvement by the homemaker that was achieved in the first instance in connection with the outdoorsperson.

In another case, the client was manufacturing and selling a shoulder mount for scopes and cameras fitted with large telephoto lenses. The device looked like the stock of an automatic rifle, but with a camera attachment in lieu of a gun barrel. It was to be used in place of a tripod for better mobility, the shoulder stock providing an added degree of support and stability. The market was defined as a class of individuals who use professional photographic or optical equipment in the field. These were typified by outdoor photographers, ornithologists and other wildlife animal watchers and hunters, border patrol or FBI agents, and other law enforcement personnel doing field surveillance. A proposed promotional brochure featured the photograph of a man in camouflage gear partly hidden in thick foliage and holding the device to be named equipped with a powerful scope. This scene lead to the conception of a television commercial in a safari-style setting in which the observer would grab his camera-fitted XYZ mount to aim at a fluttering flock of exotic birds rising from a swamp. The final scene showed the resulting sharp picture of a bird in flight. The gist of the commercial was to demonstrate the rapidity and accuracy obtained by the use of the product in a difficult field environment. The message was distilled to a short phrase: sharpness in the field. But before pursuing this exemplary case, it might be advisable to define the elements that come into play in the final translation of the message into a commercial name.

CHAPTER 9

NUTS AND BOLTS

It is now time to get down to the nuts and bolts of commercial name formation. Once the message has been reduced to a simple theme or image, the final step is to devise a word or short phrase that carries the theme or conveys the image, one that can act as a commercial name. The name may be borrowed in toto from our rich English vocabulary or from any other language, or it may be partially or entirely fabricated from word fragments assembled in a totally new fashion. The former method is explained in this chapter. The latter is the subject of Chapter 10.

BORROWING THE NAME

Borrowing an entire word or phrase from English or another language offers the most direct and oftentimes the most effective way to name a company, product, or service. Words and phrases are selected for the impression they make upon the mind of the customer, as is explained in Chapter 1. That impression results from the symbolism, metonymy, evocation, onomatopoeic effect, and aesthetic or humorous qualities implicit in that word or phrase.

SYMBOLISM

The simplest and most effective way to convey an idea, short of direct description, is to use symbolic terms. Symbolism is the expression of an abstract concept by way of a concrete or tangible substitute. The practice is as old as humankind and common to all ages and cultures. The most primitive and still the most effective symbols are animals. Animals were the most common symbols in medieval heraldry and remain the favorite components of modern trademarks. The lions in William the Conqueror's coat of arms and in the Metro Goldwyn Mayer logo convey the same message of strength and superiority. The ant and the bee are symbols of industry, the bull expresses combativeness, the dove is a peace messenger, and the owl signifies wisdom.

The world of the automobile is replete with animal allegories. Besides JAGUAR and COUGAR, discussed earlier, we find CHEETAH, SPIDER, SCORPION, IMPALA, SKYHAWK, FIRE-HAWK, SUNBIRD, THUNDERBIRD, ARONDE (French for "Swallow"), TAURUS, MIURA (a breed of Andalusian fighting bulls), BRAHMA, and CAMARGUE (a breed of Provençal fighting bulls and ponies).

Common flora are another abundant source of symbols. The oak tree stands for strength, the lily exudes purity, the rose proclaims beauty, while the violet suggests humility. The world of fashion perfumes and cosmetics shows a predilection for that type of name, as demonstrated by the brands FLEURS DE RO-CAILLE, LILAC LADY, LILY PADS, NIGHT FUCHSIA, ROSE-BUDS, ROSEFAIR, and SHY VIOLET.

These are only a few examples from a large pool of basic symbols available to the semonemician. A higher level of symbolism consists of creating new signs to represent complex ideas. Prime examples are the use of letters and syllables to denote sounds, words to picture things, musical notes to evoke melody and pitch, signs to express mathematical operations, and commercial names to identify companies or their products. Thus, commercial semonemics, which seeks to create names rather than definitions as labels, is essentially rooted in symbolism. Indeed, symbolism was the basic technique used in coining such famous names as GREYHOUND and JAGUAR. The use of symbols is the most direct and practical way to avoid legally impermissible definitions in the selection of commercial names.

Keep in mind, however, that the use of a common symbol to designate the goods or the activity of a company may still result in a description rather than a name and, as such, be plagued with all the legal impediments inherent to descriptive terms. The name CORNUCOPIA applied to a general store was found to be unprotectible against the use of the same term within the same community for a shopping center food mall. The court ruled that CORNUCOPIA was a common description for something dispensing a variety of edible goods.

METONYMY

Metonymy is a figure of speech that uses the name of one thing for that of another associated with or suggested by it. A common example of metonymy is the use of the phrase "White House" in lieu of "the president." One way to avoid purely descriptive designations is through metonymic generalization. For instance, a noun is substituted for an adjective; or the name of the object's common user, the object's location, or its field of use is selected to designate the object itself. It would not be possible to sell a car under the vocable FAMOUS or POPULAR, but the synonym of fame and popularity—CELEBRITY—constitutes an acceptable name. In CRAFTSMAN, the name of the user serves to designate a brand of tools. The same technique was applied in selecting the name COVER GIRL for a line of cosmetics. CUISINART describes the field of use for a food processor. Notice that CELEBRITY conveys the same message as FAMOUS or POPULAR while avoiding a merely descriptive characterization. The marks CRAFTSMAN and COVER GIRL have the added merit of presenting a highly motivating role model to the potential buyer.

ALLUSION OR EVOCATIVE REFERENCE

A commercial name also may be based on an **evocative reference** to something that brings to mind an appropriate set of images or sensations. We discussed earlier how the mark HANG TEN refers to the sport of surfing and how the name SHASTA evokes a snow-covered peak. In the files of Alias is also found

PUMPHOUSE

the mark PUMPHOUSE for surfing equipment. To a dedicated surfing enthusiast, this name clearly alludes to a piece of surfing lore.

The reference technique can powerfully pack a commercial name with broad imagery. Its effectiveness depends upon the proper choice of that key word that will open a floodgate of evocations and feelings in the mind of the targeted customer. When a reference is used to identify a company, product, or service addressed to a limited audience, it acts as a password to the private psyche of the individual and establishes an instant kinship between the individual and that company, product, or service. This phenomenon was effectively employed in the creation of the mark CHAPULIN, which was addressed to a certain class of Hispanics.

History and mythology offer a vast pool of illustrious names, great deeds, and famous places, the utilization of which can make a very eloquent and inspiring name. BENJAMIN FRANKLIN POSTAL CENTER, JOHN HANCOCK MUTUAL LIFE INSURANCE COMPANY, CAESARS PALACE, MARATHON, and BRANDYWINE are all examples of commercial names based on historical **allusions.** Geography also can be a source of allusive vocables that are loaded with enticing imagery, such as SEVEN SEAS LODGE and ACAPULCO POOLS.

ONOMATOPES

Onomatopes are words formed with syllables that suggest the sound associated with their meaning. The English speech is particularly rich in onomatopes, the like of *applause, bumblebee, chickadee, drop, ebullition, flail, gag, hawk, jingle, knock, lock, mewl, owl, pop, peck, plunk, prick, quack, reel, sputter, stutter, tinkle, wallop,* and *zip,* just to name a few. These words are excellent examples of effective use of suggestive sounds in word formation. As explained earlier, there is a difference between the meaning of a word and the engram that the word leaves in the mind of the person hearing or reading it for the first time. The meaning may be totally arbitrary, as the result of a long and complex derivation from an obscure source. Take the word *pest,* for example. During childhood, we learn that *pest* designates an insect or a rodent, and in some cases, figuratively, somebody or something annoying. Aside from these learned meanings, the term is rather empty and dull. By contrast, the word *bumblebee,* in addition to designating a particular insect (the learned meaning), talks to our mind by way of onomatopes to conjure the lazy image of the buzzing insect bumping into things. In this way, the use of onomatopoeic syllables can greatly enhance the impact of a name. We also discovered this phenomenon in the joyous jingling sound conveyed by the service mark JELLIBEANS.

RHYTHM AND POETRY

A skilled semonemician has to be somewhat of a poet. The rhythmic cadence of a name can greatly affect the name's appeal and memorability. The mark COCA-COLA may have had some serious legal shortcomings, evidenced by the unchallengeable subsequent emergence of the closely related competitive marks PEPSI COLA and RC COLA, but the famous name retains a tremendous aural impact and high profile, mainly because of its balanced rhythm. The name hits the mind like recurring waves of surf crashing against a rocky shore.

A certain degree of attention-getting can be conferred on a word by giving it a last syllable that differs from most conven-

tional endings found in English. Names ending with *-aire,
-i, -o,* or *-a* have a definite foreign flavor. You should be careful,
however, when ending a name with *-o* or *-a.* These vowels are
usually atonic in Romance languages, except in French, where
they are heavily accentuated. Hispanics also tend to stress a
final *i.* The pronunciation of such a name may therefore vary
with the ethnic background of the individual and, as a result,
assume a variety of meanings. The possible interpretation by
Spanish-speaking people of the name NOVA for an automobile
as one that "does not work" has already been mentioned.

All of the phonetic techniques available to a poet for creating
cadence or impact, softness or harshness, can be used to invent
a commercial name. Alliterations, as used in COCA-COLA and
CASCADE, are powerful ways to impart cadence to a name.
Judicious alternation of short and long syllables and careful
accentuation can be used to convey the exact feeling or image
that matches the commercial message, as we have already seen
in the name JELLIBEANS.

Rhymes and symmetry can also enhance the appeal of a
name. A good example is the famous brand name FRUIT OF
THE LOOM. The English language in this respect is a very
malleable medium, offering greater diversity and versatility than
French or Spanish. The mark COCA-COLA, when uttered by a
Frenchman, sounds flat and monotonous. (This might be the
reason why Dr. Pemberton's elixir has never made great inroads
among the French people!) But who can blame them for prefer-
ring a bottle of DOM PERIGNON, a brand name of champagne
that sounds as good when pronounced by a Frenchman as by an
Englishman.

You should avoid syllables and phonemes that are not commonly encountered in English and upon which, while the mind
hesitates, the vocal organs totter, trip, and stutter. Such names
as MUMPSVAX and RUMPELSTILTSKIN, both found on the
Federal Register of Trademarks, make interesting tongue twisters but poor commercial identifiers.

You may want to use the artifice of strange spelling to impart some character or exoticism to a name. For example, in
naming a brand of sweaters made from Scottish or Welsh wool,
you may want to use one of those Gaelic-sounding words with
an intriguing sequence of consonants, like GWRI or MYRDDIN.

However, keep in mind that names that are hard to pronounce are also hard to remember.

Although rhythm, sonority, fluidity, and other aesthetic attributes of a commercial name enhance the name's efficiency, they constitute a mere surface treatment of little substance without a strong marketing and legal underpinning. The true value of a name resides in its distinctiveness. To select a commercial name on the basis of its phonetic quality alone is no wiser than using a surname to satisfy one's ego. These two blindfolded approaches only invite problems.

HUMOR

The impact and memorability of a commercial name can sometimes benefit from a little dose of witticism or humor. This is particularly true when the thing to be named is a consumer product or one addressed to a youthful audience. There was some humor in the coining of HANG TEN for surfers' T-shirts and L'EGGS for panty hose and a bit of witticism in the creation of the play on words CHAIN OF COMMAND. Another amusing play on words is the naming of a brand of auxiliary engines designed to facilitate docking of a yacht into a narrow berth as SIDEKICK.

Humorous names are friendly. They immediately establish a rapport or sympathetic relationship between the company, product, or service, and the customer. They are good for public relations. Subtle humor definitely has a role to play, albeit a limited one, in commercial semonemics.

The Federal Register of Trademarks lists many amusing marks. A few of them are recalled for your entertainment, without advancing an opinion as to their effectiveness or good taste: BACKSEAT SALLY for a musical group, BANANA REPUBLIC for a chain of casual and safari-style clothing outlets, FUNDERWEAR for underwear, SOCIAL SECURITY for colognes and deodorants, JOGSTRAP for a clutch used by runners to carry weights or a beverage container, and DERMA LA DOUCHE, which needs no explanation.

Humor is often achieved at the expense of a particular individual, group (ethnic or otherwise), or organization. Be wary of stepping on anybody's toes when creating a witty name, or you may find yourself the defendant in a multi-count lawsuit. Do not try to capitalize on the reputation of some celebrity. The most parodic and facetious creation, no matter how clever and amusing, will not be allowed for commercial use if it takes advantage of, or reflects adversely upon, the reputation of another individual or company. Use of the name GARBAGE PAIL KIDS for a set of humorous cards depicting caricatures of the famous CABBAGE PATCH doll characters was readily enjoined. Comedian Johnny Carson was able to stop Here's Johnny Portable Toilets, Inc. from using the famous introductory line to his "Tonight" show in connection with the defendant's business of renting and selling portable toilets. To make sure that the public would not miss the allusion, the defendant, after its HERE'S JOHNNY trademark, had added for good measure the qualifying phrase "The World's Foremost Commodian."

It is noteworthy that the decision in favor of Johnny Carson was not based on any grounds of invasion of privacy or other attempt to demean the person and reputation of the plaintiff, but on the likelihood of public confusion between the source of the portable toilets and the line of garments sold under the mark HERE'S JOHNNY by Johnny Carson Apparel, Inc., as well as the HERE'S JOHNNY RESTAURANTS.

APPLICATION

It is now appropriate to return to the naming of the portable scope or camera shoulder mount discussed in Chapter 7. We were about to translate the distilled commercial message of an optically sharp instrument in the adverse outdoors environment.

The type of potential buyers—namely, hunters, law enforcement agents, bird-watchers, and outdoor photographers—pointed to utilizing the common English class of vocabulary. This was not the place to rely on learned etymology but upon some everyday words. Simple and direct symbolism was the means selected to convey the optical sharpness. The words *eagle, falcon,* and *hawk* appeared as likely candidates. Of those three terms, only *hawk* had some onomatopoeic quality to reflect the cry of the fleeing flock. But if the sharp vision of the hawk is proverbial, the image was seen as somewhat of a cliché. The dilemma was resolved by creating a new breed of hawk, called the BUSH-HAWK. The prefix *Bush* is straight out of the television commercial and conveys the outdoors setting perfectly. The two successive *h*'s lend additional distinction to the name, just as two *x*'s do in the name EXXON. The stress that is placed on the first syllable, combined with the hard sound of the final k, gives sufficient impact to the word to make it stand out clearly in the flow of speech. BUSHHAWK has many other obvious qualities. It is short, simple, somewhat familiar, and therefore friendly. In fact, the word is so familiar that one accepts it readily at first as a common word, but in a split second the mind questions that apparent familiarity and then soon decides that there is no such thing as a bushhawk. These mental gymnastics further embed the name into the mind and contribute to its memorability.

CHAPTER 10

COINING THE NAME

Coining a brand new commercial name involves a far more complex process than forming that name from one or more borrowed words. But the process offers greater flexibility of expression, and with a little experience, can yield the highest grade of commercial identities.

New terms are continuously created by lexicologists to identify scientific and technological developments. This name-creation process is done with a certain concern for universality and ease of communication between scientists of different language backgrounds. The new words follow certain conventions about the choice of etymological roots and orthography. Semonemics can also follow the same conventions, but with a totally different perspective. The semonemician's goal is not to define a new object or concept in universally acceptable terms, but to promote a company or its product or services.

In this chapter, we review the conventional principles of word generation, such as composition, derivation, analogy, and etymological sources, but with a marked bias toward the mercantile purpose of commercial names.

COMPOSITION

By far the simplest and most primitive technique of commercial name formation consists of joining two or more entire words, a process called **composition.** This was done in a somewhat sophomoric manner with the creation of such names as KITCHEN-AID, ADJUSTASTROKE, and WATERPIK, and with more savvy in MOONDANCE, RAINBIRD, WINDBLOSSOMS, and PALM-OLIVE. The names in the first set tend to be descriptive, flat, and uninspiring. The names in the second set are more whimsical and distinctive. We have already discussed an excellent example of composition in BUSHHAWK (Chapter 9).

Resist the temptation to imitate such names as ADJUSTA-STROKE, ADJUSTA-POISE, ADAPT-A-SWITCH, DIAL-A-LITE, PLUG-O-MATIC, TOUCH-O-MATIC, and other clumsily articulated descriptions. Avoid hyphens in composite names because they tend to break up an otherwise fanciful term into descriptive segments, thus weakening its distinctiveness. Hyphenation sometimes looks awkward and is often dropped by copywriters and typesetters, which, in turn, results in the confusing use of various versions of the same name. The names KOOL-AID, VITA-LIFE, and SUN-DROP could be advantageously changed to KOOLAID, VITALIFE, and SUNDROP. Hypenation would greatly disparage the beautifully coined name SUNKIST.

The composition process, which is just one step above plain borrowing of an existing term, can utilize symbolism or evocative reference and is subject to all the rules discussed in Chapter 9. It results, however, in a new term, and as such, may benefit from a higher degree of distinctiveness than a name that is merely borrowed.

FUSION

Going one step further, **fusion** is the process of bonding two or more words by overlapping similar portions in those words. BUSHHAWK could have been fused into BUSHAWK. The expressive term GRASPEN was coined by fusion of the words *grasp* and *aspen* as a trademark for a ski-carrying clutch, with obvious reference to the famous Colorado ski resort.

Fusion usually produces a concise name that carries the impressions and meanings of two or more component words, as illustrated by the following examples:

MONITORQUE   from *monitor* and *torque*
MAXIMAGE   from *maxima* and *image*

FUNDERWRITER   from *fund* and *underwriter*
PERFORMULA   from *perform* and *formula*
ASTRALLIANCE   from *astral* and *alliance*
SUBURBANK   from *suburb* and *bank*

TACKING AND CLIPPING

Tacking, also called derivation, consists of adding a prefix or a suffix to a borrowed word, as in PAN AMERICAN, MICRO-PHASE, and FASHIONETTE.

You should not limit your choice of prefixes and suffixes to the conventional *pan-, micro-,* and *-ette* used in the previous examples. Commercial nomenclature is full of examples that have been carved out of such words as *flex* from *flexible, tex* from *textile* or *text, tech* from *technique, matic* from *automatic, perma* from *permanent, porta* from *portable,* and *pro* from *professional.* The prefix *pro* is sometimes ambiguous, as it can mean either "professional," "ahead of," "in lieu of," "on behalf of," or "in favor of." Thus, the actual meanings of the names PRO-SLIDE and PRO-TEK are not very clear. As a suffix, however, *pro* clearly stands for "professional."

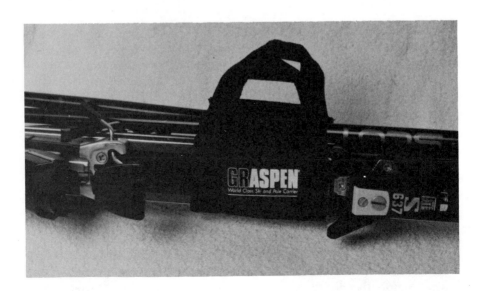

Clipping, also referred to as retrogressive or back formation, is the opposite of tacking, in that the beginning or ending of a word is shorn away, as was done in AUTOMAT and PAN AM. The result is usually a new term that retains the impression and meaning of the root but is more distinctive.

Clipping accounts for the formation of many contemporary terms, such as *mob* from *mobile*. *Mobile* is an abbreviation for the Latin phrase *mobile vulgus,* which means "a fluid throng." *Cab* was derived from *cabriolet,* and *van* used to be *caravan.* Recently, CARAVAN has returned as a brand name for a minivan.

Clipping often results from an instinctive search for conciseness that manifests itself primarily at the expense of complex words. *Curiosity* was shortened to *curio,* and *influenza* to *flu.* Sometimes, only the accentuated syllables are retained, as *coon* for *raccoon.*

In certain circles, clipping is a snobbish affectation. It would not be *hip* (from *hipster*) to use the word *beauty* when one can say *beaut.* VETTE stands for the racy automobile CORVETTE, and JAG is used in lieu of JAGUAR. Among teenagers, clipping is often a fad (a term probably clipped from a regional British dialect). The soda-pop mark FANTA from *fantastic* is right on target.

MIMICKING MONIKERS

The phrase mimicking monikers refers to various types of coined words that are little more than borrowed words in disguise. The disguise may be an altered spelling, as in HOLSUM, or the addition or substitution of one or more letters. The Upjohn Company added one letter to the word *regain* to create a mark for the baldness treatment lotion REGAINE. The table game STRATEGO and the JELL-O brand of desserts are two of many commercial names formed by substituting or tacking on the letter *o* to the end of a common English word.

You should never mimic a word that is a generic or a common descriptive term for the company, product, or service you are trying to name. If your creation sounds like that generic or commonly descriptive term, it will be treated as an unprotectible name, regardless of the way you spell or misspell it. Henri's Food

Products Company, Inc. had sold more than $10 million worth of its HENRI'S TAS-TEE DRESSING brand of pourable salad dressing when Tasty Snacks, Inc. began offering a line of TASTY Russian dressing, TASTY Italian dressing, and TASTY mayonnaise. Henri's sued Tasty for infringement. The court granted Tasty a summary judgment dismissing the complaint after finding that TAS-TEE was as generic and commonly descriptive as the term *tasty* and could not be protected. The 7th Circuit Court of Appeal has since upgraded TAS-TEE to the level of a merely descriptive name and remanded the case to the trial court for reconsideration in light of this new finding. This is small consolation to the plaintiff in that it only results in a costly prolongation of its frustrating and futile legal attempt to protect its ill-chosen name. Jurists tend to disregard the fanciful spelling of a commercial name and to treat it as the conventionally written phonetic equivalent, on the questionable assumption that commercial names are more often heard than seen.

A certain degree of distinctiveness can be conferred upon a merely descriptive name, however, by a touch of whimsy in its spelling. That kernel of originality might be sufficient to launch the name toward a long and distinguished career. Names like RICE KRISPIES and PREST-O-LITE have already proved that point.

Avoid adopting the corrupted spelling of a competitor's name; for example, you could not get away with a CODAC or a KANON for cameras. B WEAR was found to be confusingly similar to BEE WEAR, and SEYCOS for watches was ruled impermissibly close to SEIKO. Here again, however, while the exact phonetic equivalent of a competitor's name cannot be tolerated, a fanciful spelling may nudge a borderline imitator into a noninfringing zone. The name WUV's for a restaurant was found to be distinguishable from LOVE's. Common sense and alertness to the likelihood of confusion should be your guides when coining mimicking monikers.

ANALOGY

Comedian Victor Borge always had an unorthodox way with words. He once announced that he wanted to retire into a monkery, explaining that, if nuns live in a nunnery, monks must gather in a monkery! If the word *monastery* did not exist, Borge's pun would be pointless—just another application of a modern word-coining technique called **analogy.** That technique is responsible for the word *motorcade,* created by analogy to *cavalcade. Motorcade,* in turn, inspired the name ASPENCADE for a motorcycle rally. The special habitat reserved for the breeding of the endangered California condor at the San Diego Wild Animal Park was baptized CONDORMINIUM, obviously prompted by the term *condominium.* EMPIRIN mimics the now generic term ASPIRIN, and LAUNDROMAT imitates AUTOMAT. MINUTEMAID was forged by analogy to *minuteman,* as NUMBERJACK was by *lumberjack.* ICE CAPADE was coined by analogy to *escapade,* a breakaway or wild adventure. Thus, the term ICE CAPADE is semantically equivalent to the name HOLIDAY ON ICE. As in the tacking process, the name conveys the impressions and meanings of both the root (*condor, laundry,* or *ice*) and the imitation (*condominium, automat,* or *escapade*).

SEMANTATION

Semantation is the semonemic version of what lexicologists call combination—the formation of a word with elements taken from other words. For example, *smog* is a combination of elements taken from *smoke* and *fog.* Lewis Carroll coined the term *portmanteau* (French for "coatrack") to designate this type of word. On a portmanteau word are metaphorically hung several parts of other words, just like pieces of clothing on a coatrack. In a similar manner, semantation involves a combination of expressive word segments that seeks to preserve the semantic contents of the borrowed elements.

Let us begin by dissecting some common English words into their smallest meaningful components (called **morphemes** by linguists). There are three components in the word *computing:* the prefix *com* (from the Latin *cum,* "together"), the root *put* (from the Latin *putare,* "to think"), and the gerund ending *ing.* The word *cap* (from the Latin *capa,* "hood") has only one component, but the word *caps* has two: the radix *cap* and the plural ending *s.*

The endings *ing* and *s* serve only the morphological functions of indicating an ongoing action in one case and plurality in the other. They are of little interest to the name-maker. By contrast, the other components fulfill a more significant role of communicating some information or meaning. They are called semes by linguists and **semants** in semonemics, a back form of semantemes (from the Greek *semainein,* "to signify, to transmit a signal"). In other words, semants are the basic message carriers found in the words of a language. The semants *tres* and *trans* as in *trespass* and *transport* are equivalent and mean *across.* The semant *acu* as in *acute* and *acupuncture* implies something sharp or pointed. The semants *bum* and *bom,* as in *bumbling* and *bomb,* convey an explosive sound.

Just as in the game SCRABBLE, lettered tiles can be lined up to form a word, then scrambled and recombined to form others; words can be dismantled into semants, and those semants can be scrambled and rearranged to create new meaningful words through the process of semantation. The source of those dismantleable words may be English or some other etymologically related language.

The structure of the mark LUCITE shows a good application of this semantation process. The radix *luci* is derived from the genitive form *lucis* of *lux* (Latin for "light"), appearing in such words as *lucid* and *lucigen.* Thus, the semant *luci* connotes something clear or bright. The suffix *ite* appears in many mineral names, such as *pyrite, anthracite,* and *dolomite.* By combining the two semants *luci* and *ite* severed from other words, the new name LUCITE was created, conveying the image of a clear or bright solid material. Other examples of semantation are shown in Figure 10–1.

You should always strive to combine this method of name fabrication with some of the expression-enhancing techniques discussed in Chapter 9—sympiptism, symbolism, evocative reference, onomatopoeia, rhythm, and, when called for, humor. In the coining of SCENFOLI, illustrated in Figure 10–1, there is a sympiptic effect due to the soft sound of the first semant *scent,* the mellifluous sound of the second semant *foli,* and the fragrant image conveyed by each component. The name also produces an onomatopoeic rendition of a soft wind through foliage. The early

FIGURE 10–1
Examples of Semantation.

Goods: Pedal-Powered Four-Wheel Surreys for Rental in the Beach Cities
         of Southern California and the Island of Santa Catalina.

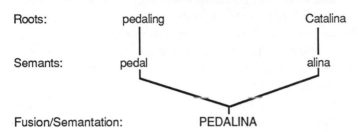

Roots: pedaling   Catalina

Semants: pedal   alina

Fusion/Semantation: PEDALINA

Business: Flower Shop

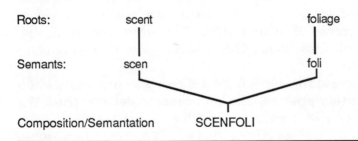

Roots: scent   foliage

Semants: scen   foli

Composition/Semantation   SCENFOLI

accentuation and soft ending endow the word with a harmonious
cadence.

   You should begin to appreciate at this point the important
role that semantation plays in the semonemic arts. It is only
through its mastery and the acquisition of a broad vocabulary
base that you can become a skillful commercial namesmith.

IDEOPHONES

In addition to semants shorn from other words, you can create
name-building components with **ideophonemes,** also called
ideophones. These are letters or syllables that do not rise to

the level of bona fide semants in the language, yet they can convey thoughts and feelings in a very subtle, sometimes subconscious, way. The combination *sl,* for example, which appears in *slice, slick, slide,* and *slip,* suggests a gliding or sliding movement. Linguists have, on occasion, referred to this phenomenon with such unwieldy designations as phonestheme, phonosememe, and phonological syntagmeme.

In Chapter 1, the evocative power of the plosive dental and guttural consonants was demonstrated in the macho names TIGER and COUGAR for sporty automobiles. Sibilant and liquid consonants can be exploited to suggest softness, as in SILKEASE. In practically every language, the maternal vocable includes the nasal *m* sound. This letter may be used to connote maternal tenderness, as was done with the MOMAR and MONAVE brands of perfumes. Youth and joy are rendered with affricates (*j, ch, g*) and **glides** or semivowels (*y, w*), as in JOYA, JOVAN, YOLAI, and YU. Imaginative arrangement of consonants and unconventional diphthongs can yield such intriguing and attention-getting handles as XEROX, EXXON, TKO, and ZZOTTI. Don't be afraid to explore the most hidden corner of your psyche to find forceful ideophones and to use them effectively in bold name-coining exercises.

MULTIMEDIA NAMES

Combinations of several of the previously discussed techniques can also achieve effective results. The corporate name CALIBAKER for an industrial bakery concern combines clipping (*Cali* from *California*) and composition (*Cali* plus *baker*). PEDALINA involves the semantation of the semants *pedal* and *alina,* as well as the fusion of their respective segments—*al* and *-al-.* CHAIN OF COMMAND uses an allusion to the military hierarchy and a play on words to attract attention. PUMPHOUSE demonstrates the buttressing of an allusion to a book about surfing—*The Pumphouse Gang* by Tom Wolf—with sympiptism achieved by the onomatopoeic rendering of the pumping sound: pump! house!, pump! house! Allusion and analogy are the techniques used to coin the name ASPENCADE. Diversity in the choice and combination of techniques and the broad selection of semantic elements yields the most eloquent commercial identifiers.

The pool of name-building material is varied and inexhaustible. In the next chapter, we examine some of its most accessible components.

CHAPTER 11

CONSTRUCTION MATERIAL

Forming a new commercial name can be considered analogous to the construction of a building. The builder can go to the quarry to cut new stones for the walls and to the forest to fell some lumber for the roof. Similarly, the commercial namesmith can go back to the traditional etymological sources to carve out new semants from which to coin the name. But the name-maker could instead borrow semants from contemporary languages, just as the house-builder can scavenge old structures for used bricks, stones, and rafters. In either case, old and new materials can be combined to achieve a striking stylistic feature for the new building or to give more incisiveness to a name. To carry the analogy a step further, the construction of a dwelling house and of a commercial establishment are each subject to unique requirements that may dictate different choices of materials. In the same way, the coining of commercial names is based upon certain principles that differ substantially from those of ordinary lexicology.

QUARRY STONES

The **etymology** of a word is its derivation from roots in one or more languages. This derivation may be historical and due to natural evolution of the term through continued use by successive generations, or learned if scholars coined or borrowed the word from a parent idiom to designate some new development or discovery. The history of the word *salad* starts with the Latin *sal*, meaning "salt," which gave *salata*, meaning "salted." Medieval Provençal changed the *t* into *d* to make it *salada*, which the French adopted and turned into *salade*. The Norman invasion brought the word to England, where it took its modern form of *salad*. The three historically documented ancestor languages in this example, along with a few other idioms, offer a vast pool of semants from which to form new names.

Latin itself has its roots in older and generally scantily documented tongues, such as Etruscan, all the way back to the Proto-Indo-European language from which most Eastern Asiatic and European vernaculars are derived. These older idioms have nothing to offer to the semonemician. Latin, however, borrowed heavily from Greek, its older Indo-Europe cousin. From Latin, English inherited many Greek words. The Greek verb *kubernein,* meaning "to steer a boat" or "to govern," became *gubernare* in Latin, then *gouverner* in French, and finally *to govern* in English. It is also from Greek that many learned words are coined. The modern term *cybernetics,* which is the study of complex electronic thinking machines, is based on the same Greek word *kubernein* that is at the origin of *governor.* Thus, we have both a popularly derived word (*to govern*) and a learned term (*cybernetics*) with the same Greek root; their meanings, however, are quite different. There is also a significant difference in their levels of intelligibility to people with varied educational backgrounds. The popularly derived word *to govern* can be understood by a far greater segment of the public than the scholastic term *cybernetics.*

Over the last two centuries, Greek has become the most prolific source of word-building material to be used by a myriad of new sciences and technologies, from *photography, cinematography,* and *radiography,* to *kinetics, statistics,* and *cybernetics;* from *gram, liter,* and *meter,* to *ion, neutron,* and *cyclotron.* This borrowing process is of such an increasing magnitude that Greek-based terms have become about as numerous in modern English as the original Anglo-Saxon words. Because the roots of the old Anglo-Saxon language and its close ancestors are poorly documented, scholars borrow little from that stock to form new words. But this source of semants is not off-limits to the commercial name-maker, who should not be afraid to dip into the Anglo-Saxon lexicon, where powerful name-building elements can be found.

But first, let us walk for a while in the footsteps of lexicologists who have limited their etymological quarries to Greek, Latin, French, and the few other Romance languages, namely Italian, Provençal, and Spanish, that have made important contributions to the development of English. Many of the prefixes and suffixes derived from those parent languages can help to build some effective names. Some of the prefixes and suffixes most commonly used in semonemics are:

From Greek	Meaning	Example
a-, an-	Privative	Anacin
anti-	Against	Antiphrine
auto-	Self	Automat
bio-	Life	Biochem
dia-	Through	Diaguide
pan-	All	Pan American
poly-	Many	Polymerin
tele-	Remote	Telemart
syn-	Together	Syntron
-dyne	Force	Teledyne
-lite	Stone	Bakelite

From Latin	Meaning	Example
ad-	Toward	Adazine
com-	Together	Compal
e, ex-	Out of	Exidol
omni-	All	Omnifax
trans-	Through	TransAmerica
vita-	Life	Vitalis
-ator	Agent	Kelvinator

From French	Meaning	Example
-et, -ette	Diminutive	Casualets
		Fashionette

From Provençal	Meaning	Example
-ada, -ade	The act or product of participation in	Gatorade Aspencade

Components from learned sources, other than common prefixes and suffixes, should be used sparingly in creating new words because they can only be appreciated or even recognized by literate individuals. While they are almost mandatory in the creation of names directed to scientists and scholars, they should be avoided when forging names that must reach those individuals who did not have the benefit of a college education. How many people can see something bright and shiny in the mark FORMICA? Yet, that is what *mica* (from the Latin *micare*, "to sparkle") is trying to convey.

Name-makers should use only the most familiar etymological roots that can be found in contemporary English if they want to reach a broad audience. Some roots have maintained a strong cohesiveness over thousands of years of use by various cultures before pervading contemporary idioms. They make ideal building blocks for new names. Let us look at the ancient radix *cap-*, from which Latin made *caput,* meaning "head," and *capa,* meaning "hooded garment." *Caput* became *cap* in Provençal, meaning "head" but also "headland"; hence, the English *cape* as in *Cape Cod.* Provençal also created *capussar,* meaning "to dive head first," which gave us *capsize.* The French from *capa* gave us *cape,* the garment from which *cap,* the headgear, evolved. But there are more: *Capitol, capital, capitalism, capitate, recapitulate,* and many other words inferring the head of something, either literally or figuratively, include this *cap* root.

With a certain disdain for Anglo-Saxon word stock and similar popular roots, most scholars and commercial name-makers prefer to draw from the erudite but more esoteric Greek and Latin terminology. The process is sometimes carried to bizarre excesses and produces such words as *treiskaidecaphobia* (fear of the number thirteen) and the unwieldy but picturesque *sesquipedalianism* (addiction to the use of long—literally, foot-and-a-half long—words). On the commercial side, we find names like HYBRINETICS, INDUCTOSYN, TELOPHASE, XYTRONYX, CHLOR-TRIMETON, and other hermetic tongue twisters. Hermetic is used to describe these names because the names are tightly sealed from our understanding; their message can only be understood by a few informed individuals. A hermetic name is like a clamshell that hides the nature and quality of its contents. A good commercial identifier should be like a showcase, extolling rather than concealing the product, service, or company it designates.

The use of learned Latin and Greek roots in coining scientific nomenclature is understandable and even praiseworthy since it results in a consistent and universal terminology that facilitates exchanges between scholars and scientists of different cultures. The coining of commercial names, however, cannot be based on such an idealistic concern for universalism, or on any other altruistic concept. It must respond to the demands of the marketplace and the challenge of the competition. Its foremost objective is to motivate the consumer. This can hardly be accomplished with names created from obscure Greek or Latin roots.

USED BRICKS

Learned scientific jargon is not very effective in reaching the heart and mind of the average customer. By contrast, the English language and particularly Anglo-Saxon terms, with their short and incisive terminology, offer a more intelligible pool of effective words and semants, as demonstrated by such names as AMBERLITE, MR GOODWRENCH, PLAYSKOOL, RAINBIRD, and SUNKIST.

Contemporary literary English shows a marked preference for monosyllabic or disyllabic words of Saxon origin, such as *blast, blot, dig, doom, gag, mess, proud, sap,* and *trust,* compared to their more elaborate synonyms derived from Greek, Latin, or some Romance tongue: *detonation, obliterate, excavation, condemn, restrain, confusion, arrogant, undermine,* and *confidence.* Mario Pei has attributed this phenomenon to the influence of the press, where printing space is at a premium and to editors and copywriters, who must convey as much information as possible in a limited column space. Others blame television and its attempt to reach the lowest common level of understanding among its audience.

Whatever the reason for this stylistic trend, the commercial namesmith had better follow it, for his aim is also to reach the broadest audience. This sort of return to the source of the English idiom is very democratic in character. Until the turn of the century, literary English was the domain of an educated minority. There was an elitist tendency to select a learned term, such as *appanage,* over a more common synonym, such as *realm* or *domain,* or *calembour* in lieu of *pun.* This ivory-tower mentality is still very much in evidence in certain circles. Listen, if you have the occasion, to the news on the B.B.C. Closer to home, most lawyers stubbornly cling to an esoteric legalese terminology. As a commercial name-maker, you cannot afford this type of behavior. Instead, you must select semants from the popular and even colloquial tongue to convey your message to a broader audience.

Compare, for instance, the expressive character of names like ALLEREST, CHERACOL, and NYQUIL, coined with contemporary word segments, to names in the same general field with a more scholastic pedigree, such as CHLOR-TRIMETON, NEOSYNEPHRIN, and SUDAFED. The broader appeal of the former terms over the latter is mainly due to the more common origin of their building elements.

The learned term FOCUS, as we saw in an earlier chapter, may not be favored as a commercial name. The implied idea of concentration and center of attention can be more eloquently conveyed by the popularly evolved name TARGET, also adopted by a chain of department stores. Furthermore, TARGET does not run the same risk as FOCUS of being grossly misinterpreted by certain individuals.

You must be careful, when coining a name from etymological elements, not to create a mere definition of the product to be named, albeit in another language. One cannot monopolize a foreign or ancient word, any more than its English version. The U.S. Patent and Trademark Office once refused to register the name MICROKERATOME for a cutting instrument used in eye surgery. The name was coined from three Greek roots: *micro,* meaning "minuscule"; *keratos,* designating a horny tissue, such as the cornea; and *tomeion,* which is the Greek word for scalpel. However, the term was perceived by the U.S. Patent and Trademark Office as a mere scientific definition of the goods and, as such, was unworthy of registration as a trademark.

You must first try to build your name with "used bricks"—borrowed words or semants—relying upon such simple techniques as symbolism, allusion, onomatopoeia, and semantation to convey the commercial message to the broadest audience. The use of new material from remote etymological sources should be reserved for those special cases in which you have targeted a narrow but sophisticated group.

FAMILY OF NAMES

When creating several commercial names for related products, you may want to indicate their kinship by using a family of names linked by a common theme or a common root. This is a very effective approach, not only for carrying the accumulated goodwill from one product to the next, but also for preempting a broader field of use for the commercial names. By giving a series of establishments or products names based on a well-defined common theme, you might be able to prevent competitors not only from using those names but also from using any other name carrying the same theme. Brand names may be related by way of a dominant semant that appears in each one of them, such as in WALKMAN and WATCHMAN, or by a common reference or analogy, such as in APPLE and MACINTOSH, or MUSTANG and PINTO. The company that sells the CASCADE cup sells two other products, called the ROCKY cup and the OZARK cup, after other mountain ranges.

BE ORIGINAL

Always keep in mind that the marketing impact and the legal clout of a commercial name depend upon its distinctiveness, that is, its originality. Not only is it impermissible to copy the names already used by other concerns, it is also very unwise to imitate their style. Do not succumb to the temptation of following the name-coining trends or fads that from time to time sweep the marketplace. The 1920s brought us an avalanche of names with the -ex ending such as KLEENEX, CUTEX, and PYREX. In more recent years, some of the most abused prefixes or suffixes have been *master, maid,* and *mate,* as in CARPETMASTER, STAINMASTER, MINUTEMAID, RUBBERMAID, CARPET-MATE, PAPERMATE, and WORKMATE. Do not add your contribution to that insipid litany.

As noted earlier, Japanese car manufacturers are particularly fond of names ending in *a,* but this makes it difficult to differentiate between the makers or even the main attributes of the SUPRA, SENTRA, STANZA, COROLLA, CORDIA, CELICA, CRESSIDA, MICRA, MAXIMA, TREDIA, and INTEGRA. The more they add to the list, the less distinctive those names become.

Originality is the momentum of a commercial name. The more originality there is, the farther will the name propel the product in the marketplace. If this is the only thing you learn from this book, and if you practice it, you will be far ahead of the pack.

CHAPTER 12

GRAPHY, DESIGN, AND LOGO

The role of a commercial name is essentially semantic. This semantic function is fulfilled aurally through the phonetic characteristics of the name, as well as visually by way of its graphic presentation. Three separate elements contribute to that presentation: the spelling of the name, its typography, and the graphic design that accompanies it. Those three elements must be in tune with the message to be conveyed.

SPELLING

Names are more often seen than heard. While the phonetic impact of a commercial name used in different countries may vary according to changes in pronunciation, its written form leaves a more consistent and meaningful impression. The spelling of a word may indicate the word's etymological source (which is not perceivable phonetically) and by the same token may convey a subtle meaning that evades the person who only hears the vocable.

The names SYMPHOLY, SINFOLY, and SCENFOLI are phonetically very close. Any difference between their respective aural impacts mainly rests with the personalities of the listeners. However, the graphic impacts of these three names are not only quite distinct from one another, but their interpretation is limited by their obvious etymologies or derivations. They create more cohesive sets of engrams in the minds of a variety of readers.

Few fail to recognize the kinship between SYMPHOLY and the word *symphony*. The Greek etymology earmarks that name for a learned audience. SYMPHOLY could befit a festival dedicated to light classical music.

SINFOLY is of a lighter vein. The morpheme *sin* and the term *foly,* as in FOLIES BERGERES, give this name an indisputably naughty character. It would be an appropriate name for a Las Vegas musical revue or for a line of sexy lingerie. It is a word that definitely belongs to the common English classification.

The words *scent* and *foliage* seem to emanate from SCENT-FOLI. The name would be becoming for a flower shop or a perfume. It is directed to the class of buyers who speak King's English.

TYPESETTING

Just as the spelling of a word can circumscribe the word's semantic impact, its typesetting style and illumination can sharply focus its meaning.

A large variety of typefaces can be used to enhance the appearance of a commercial name, and new ones are designed every day. You should explain to a graphic artist the rationale behind the selection or creation of the name and let him suggest an appropriate style of type or create one for the occasion. The type selected should not distract from the message conveyed by the name but should instead buttress it. The trade name of ROBERT KEITH & CO., INC., the creator of giant inflatable advertising displays, and the company's trademarks are rendered in fat types with rounded corners that suggest the general shape and the gigantism of that company's creations.

Many computer product manufacturers and dealers have adopted a close version of the cross-lined types that characterize the IBM logo. In doing so, they borrow a part of the prestige enjoyed by the giant company. The limit of permissibility, just as it was previously discussed in relation to the names themselves, is the likelihood of confusion that may result in the mind of the customer as to the source or sponsorship of the goods or services.

DESIGN AND LOGO

Any graphics accompanying the name must correspond very closely to the message to be conveyed. Furthermore, the design is subject to the same rules as the name itself with regard to distinctiveness and legal strength. A graphic design that describes the named product or services is fraught with the same latent defects as the generic and descriptive names discussed earlier.

A design that is nothing but the photographic representation of the named product is a generic design and cannot be monopolized. A design that represents the named product in an original artistic manner cannot monopolize the subject matter of the design, but only its original rendition. In other words, competitors can select the same subject (the description of the product), as long as they draw it in a nonconfusing manner. In Figure 12–1, the two interpretations of the same subject matter were found to be distinct enough to avoid public confusion.

A design that is merely descriptive of the product or service it identifies carries no more legal clout than a merely descriptive name. The U.S. Patent and Trademark Office refused to register the rendition of an eight ball and cue stick (shown in Figure 12–2) used by Eight Ball, Inc. in connection with its billiard parlor. The office ruled that "since the central feature or characteristic of the applicant's billiard parlor services was the availability of billiard games, the pictorial representation of the cue stick and ball merely described said feature or characteristic."

FIGURE 12–1
Two Distinct Interpretations of the Same Subject Matter.

FIGURE 12–2
Unregistrable and Merely Descriptive Pool-ball Logo.

FIGURE 12–3
Confusingly Similar Logos.

The left-hand design in Figure 12–3 had been adopted by United Distributors, Inc. in connection with services in the field of health and beauty aids. It was refused registration on the Federal Register on the grounds that it so resembled the right-hand design previously registered as a mark for moisturizing skin cream as to be likely to deceive or to cause confusion or mistake. The subject matters of the two logos are identical; while their renditions are different, they use the same graphic technique.

Most graphic artists are regrettably ignorant of this requirement for originality. They must be sensitized to the risk of infringement and should be made aware of all known competitors' logos so that they can avoid the creation of a confusing design.

A tasteful logo that combines expressive typography with an imaginative design can boost the distinctiveness, legal clout, and marketing value of a commercial name. The mark BUSH-HAWK for a portable scope or camera shoulder mount discussed earlier was eloquently enhanced by the logo shown in Figure 12–4.

FIGURE 12–4
Expressive Logo Rendition of a Distinctive Name.

In a borderline case, the type of logo shown in Figure 12–4 could provide just the right amount of originality to place the name beyond a claim of infringement by a previous owner of an otherwise confusingly similar identifier.

CHARACTER NAMES

Whimsical characters are often used, not only as part of a logo, but also in advertising a product or service. We are all familiar with the antics of the PINK PANTHER while promoting Owens Corning building insulation material and those of MR. MAGOO on behalf of General Electric goods. Other characters are more directly connected with the company or the product they represent, such as the POPPIN' FRESH doughboy of the Pillsbury Company.

A more effective use of characters to create a memorable identifier involves giving the character's name to the company or the product, or vice versa. One may forget which brand of insulation material is promoted by the PINK PANTHER or not remember who owns POPPIN' FRESH, but there is no such confusion about DUTCH BOY paints, MR. CLEAN detergent, or JOLLY GREEN GIANT canned vegetables.

An advertising character that does not carry the name of the product is like an entertaining commercial that fails to mention the name of the goods it is supposed to promote. If the marketing plan calls for the creation of an advertising character, the selection of the character's name should be coordinated with the creation of the product name. This process is innate in the proposed name creation method described in Chapter 8, with its prerequisite formulation of an effective television commercial.

RECAPITULATION

At this time, it might be appropriate to summarize the various techniques discussed up to this point and to draw an outline of the whole semonemic process. This should help you to organize your thoughts and synthesize the teachings of this book. Figure 12–5 presents a chart that combines and organizes these teachings.

The chart is divided into four columns in which are separately listed the various semonemic techniques discussed earlier in this book, their intended effects, and the reactions they should trigger in the mind of the targeted customer. The chart shows the final result—the successful promotion of product or services—as the ultimate goal of the whole name-coining process.

The left-hand column can be used as a practical checklist of the techniques available to the name-maker for creating a new commercial name. The first block groups the methods, from symbolism to analogy, that can be applied to convey an evocative message to the consumer. Needless to say, the expression of this message is at the very heart of semonemics. Every other aspect of the name serves only to buttress this basic function.

Let us briefly review those methods. The speed, power, and machismo of sports cars are conveyed by symbolism and sympiptism in the marks COUGAR and JAGUAR. The mark STRA-TEGO mimics the word *strategy* to disclose the general nature of the game. The mark ZIPPER relies on onomatopoeia to suggest the speedy convenience of a slide fastener.

MANPOWER is a metonymic announcement of the services provided by a temporary help agency. With the name PIED PIPER, a pest-control company paints a vivid picture of its services by allusion, that is, reference, to the legendary character

FIGURE 12–5
Semonemic Techniques and Their Applications.

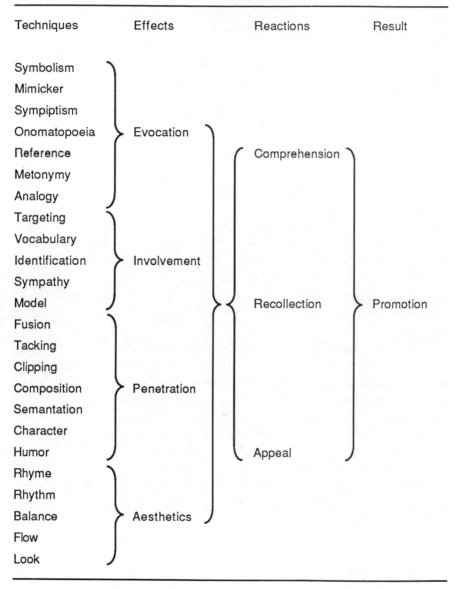

Techniques	Effects	Reactions	Result
Symbolism			
Mimicker			
Sympiptism			
Onomatopoeia	Evocation		
Reference		Comprehension	
Metonymy			
Analogy			
Targeting			
Vocabulary			
Identification	Involvement		
Sympathy			
Model		Recollection	Promotion
Fusion			
Tacking			
Clipping			
Composition	Penetration		
Semantation			
Character			
Humor		Appeal	
Rhyme			
Rhythm			
Balance	Aesthetics		
Flow			
Look			

who rid Hamelin of its rodents. It is by analogy to *motorcade* that ASPENCADE conveys the idea of a motorcycle rally among the pine forests of the southern Rockies.

In the second block are listed various approaches to reach and touch the customer. A sense of personal involvement or kinship with a company or its products can be created by carefully aiming the name toward the targeted audience, including using the most appropriate level or type of vocabulary. CHAPULIN was selected to establish a nostalgic bond with Mexican immigrants. PUMPHOUSE and HANG TEN are names with which surfers can identify. GREYHOUND plays on the sympathy of dog lovers. COVER GIRL offers a model to the young cosmetic buyer.

The penetration or incisiveness of a commercial name is the effect sought through the various name-coining techniques listed in the third block in Figure 12–5: fusion in GRASPEN, tacking in DIAGUIDE, clipping in AUTOMAT, composition in RAINBIRD, and last but not least, semantation in LUCITE and ANTIQUAX. The incisiveness of a name can be sharpened with a little touch of humor, as in CHAIN OF COMMAND, or by turning the name into a character, like the JOLLY GREEN GIANT.

Finally, the aesthetics or poetry of a commercial name can be enhanced by use of rhymes and good balance (as in FRUIT OF THE LOOM, rhythm (as in COCA-COLA), flow (as in JELLIBEANS), and even a good balanced look (as in KODAK).

All four effects—evocation, involvement, penetration, and aesthetics—work together to help the targeted consumer to understand the commercial message, remember the name, and experience some appealing thoughts upon hearing it. The final result is the successful promotion of the object named every time that the name is seen or heard.

HOLD THE VERDICT

It is not unusual, at the conclusion of a name-coining exercise, to end up with several almost equally fitting candidates. That is no time to agonize over making a final choice, since one important factor of the equation is still missing—the availability of the names.

Since the legal ownership and use of a name is predicated on priority of use in commerce, there is a substantial chance that one or more of the finalists are already preempted or will be otherwise disqualified by the results of the name-availability search. It is better, therefore, to conduct the search on all the qualifying candidates so that the outcome of the search can be used in making the final selection. Doing so may help you to avoid a great deal of disappointment and frustration, as well as the possibility of having to return to the lawyer's office in the event that the name that was painstakingly selected as the best is found to be unavailable.

CHAPTER 13

THE NAME AVAILABILITY SEARCH

In most countries that did not derive their legal system from the Common Law of England, the exclusive right to a commercial name is based on the name's entry in some national register. A name availability search can be readily performed by consulting such a register. In the United States and in a few other common-law jurisdictions, the exclusive right to the use of a distinctive trade name, trademark, or service mark (and of any confusingly similar term) is predicated upon the mark's first and continued use in commerce. There is no authoritative centralized national register that can be checked to verify whether or not a prospective name choice has not already been preempted.

Various types of registration systems exist at the state level in the United States for corporate names and marks. Most county administrations maintain registers of fictitious commercial names. Marks used in interstate and other forms of commerce regulated by the U.S. Congress may be registered with the U.S. Patent and Trademark Office under the Lanham Act. However, because these various registration systems are, for the most part, permissive and not mandatory, they reflect only a portion of the names actually in use. In general, registration by itself does not provide any ownership right but is a mere procedural advantage when attempting to enforce an already established exclusive proprietary right. In other words, a registration gives the name-owner a bigger stick to carry when going after infringers, as will be further explained a little later.

All commercial names should be searched before they are used in commerce. This rule applies to trademarks, service marks, and corporate names, as well as to fictitious business names or D.B.A.'s (acronym for "doing business as") given to partnerships and sole proprietorships. The mere adoption of a commercial name that is already used by another concern may constitute an actionable act of infringement. Commercial name-users in some of the most liberal states, such as California, are particularly at risk, since these states give precedence to the first user of a name anywhere, not just in their jurisdiction. Reserving the name with the secretary of state or having it accepted by his office does not imply that the name is available for any kind of commercial use, even as a corporate identity. California law requires that the secretary of state notify all newly organized corporations that "the filing of articles of incorporation does not of itself authorize the use of the corporate name in violation of the rights of any other person who may have acquired rights to the use of the name by reason of some other law, such as the Federal Trademark Act, California Trademark Act, Fictitious Business Name Act, and Common Law right to a trade name." Many people (and a good number of attorneys) think that the office of the secretary of state "clears" a name before reserving it or accepting it as a corporate identifier. This is not the case; the office only checks the name for direct conflict with the names of domestic corporations in good standing and those foreign corporations that are qualified to do business in the state.

In the case of the Oklahoma Osteopathic Hospital of Tulsa, mentioned in the Preface, the corporate attorney had, in fact, been asked to "clear" the name HEALTH CARE CHOICE for the health care plan. He did so by simply confirming its availability as a corporate name with the secretary of state. This procedure offered no defense when the hospital was sued for trademark infringement by Aetna Health Care Systems, Inc., the owner of the mark CHOICE for the same type of health coverage services.

How do you conduct a reliable availability search for a prospective commercial name? Before answering that question, something should be said about the common misconception that all names that are already found on corporate or trademark registers are to be declared unavailable.

The discovery of a prior registration of the prospective name by another party can be very misleading. Many registered names have been, in fact, abandoned or have not been used for so long by their one-time owners that they are presumed abandoned and free for adoption by another party. A searcher cannot rely exclusively on what is found or not found in these registers to form an opinion as to the availability of the proposed name. As explained in Chapter 5, the aura of protection ascribed to a commercial name in terms of degree of similarity, field of use, and territory depends upon its level of distinctiveness and legal strength. Accordingly, side-by-side comparison of the proposed name candidate with one previously registered, or one that is not registered but already used by someone else, can lead to a wrong conclusion if done in the abstract, that is, without taking into consideration the pertinent circumstances surrounding the use of the name by the prior owner and its intended application by the newcomer.

As you can see, an availability search involves so many complex issues that it can only be conducted effectively by a qualified professional. As the creator or prospective user of a new commercial moniker, you must clearly understand the nature of those issues so that you can make intelligent use of the search results and the accompanying professional opinion.

THE ISSUES

Four basic issues should be considered when conducting an availability search for a prospective commercial name:

1. Whether the adoption and use of the name would infringe upon the proprietary rights of another
2. Whether others can be readily prevented from adopting and using the same or a similar name
3. Whether the name can be registered on the Federal Principal Register and in other applicable jurisdictions
4. Whether the name can acquire sufficient intrinsic value to properly carry the goodwill and reputation of the business and be exploited in a lucrative manner

Each of these four issues involves a different set of criteria. None of the first three issues can be dodged without turning the search into a futile exercise. The analysis of the fourth issue, although not absolutely necessary, can be readily handled once the first three have been properly considered. Any trademark practitioner worth his salt will voluntarily discuss this issue in rendering his opinion.

Do not anticipate a black-and-white answer to any of the questions raised, and expect some gray areas. The laws and regulations controlling proprietary rights to a commercial name are so complex and subject to so many circumstantial qualifications that, except in a few rare cases, there is no absolute answer or guarantee to be had. The best that can be expected from the person conducting the search is an educated opinion that can be taken into account in making the final name choice. The soundness of this person's opinion depends entirely on his background and expertise.

A name search is not a task to assign to just any attorney, but to one with extensive experience in intellectual property matters and particularly in trademark registration and litigation. The best of the searching services can only provide lists of names gathered from various registers, without any special focus or emphasis on the issues facing the name-user. These services do not render any kind of legal opinion. The results of their work can be very misleading and are probably not worth the fee, small as it may be. If cost is a compelling factor, it is better to ask a competent practitioner to limit his search and to provide a qualified opinion at a lesser fee than to order a worthless compilation from a purely mechanical searching service.

Without getting into all the arcane rules of trademark law, let us dwell long enough on each one of the four previously listed issues to fully understand the search report and use it intelligently.

INFRINGEMENT

The primary purpose of the availability search is to obtain some assurance that the adoption of the proposed name will not expose you to infringement suits. It cannot be overemphasized that the scope of protection afforded to a commercial name depends upon the name's legal clout or distinctiveness and the likelihood of confusion that the new name may create in the mind of the customer. The fact that a name is already in use or is registered with the U.S. Patent and Trademark Office does not necessarily preclude its adoption by another. Such an adoption might, in fact, be proper for use in a different channel of commerce, especially if that first name lacks legal strength. The prior use and registration of the name CONCORD in connection with the sale of motor homes was found to be no bar to the adoption of the same name by another in connection with the sale of automobiles. The prior use of the mark DOMINO on sugar cubes did not prevent another company from adopting and using the name DOMINO'S PIZZA. The sale of an underarm antiperspirant under the name SURE could not prevent a competitor's adoption of the mark SURE & NATURAL for feminine protection shields.

On the other hand, you may be prevented from using a name that has never been used before if the name could create a likelihood of confusion with any other name, even if the name is so different that the most thorough availability search would not discover it. In Chapter 4, we saw how LOLLIPOPS was found impermissible for a skating rink over JELLIBEANS for the same type of business. Only an experienced trademark practitioner with knowledge of all the circumstances surrounding the selection of the name LOLLIPOPS could have warned its promoter about the potential conflict with the name JELLIBEANS. A mechanical availability search, commonly called an "idiot search," would have missed the potential conflict completely. It is therefore of critical importance to provide the searcher with all the pertinent information relative to the use of the proposed name and the choices of known competitors so that he can render an informed opinion.

ENFORCEABILITY

The enforceability of a new name—that is, the ability to prevent others from adopting the same or a similar name—is the other side of the coin. The adoption of a weak name may be a relatively safe approach as a protection against claims of infringement, but it is also an invitation to unpreventable future pirating by envious competitors, should the product succeed. The search may reveal some pertinent information about the prior use of the same or a similar name, about an opposition to its registration, or about some related litigation, any of which may act as a red flag to indicate a problem with the proposed name's enforceability. To obtain the most out of a search, do not hesitate to ask for some comments on that issue. Also, the search results will be more accurate if the searcher is given a clear picture of all intended and possible future applications of the name in all fields of expected use.

REGISTRABILITY

The registration of a trademark or service mark on the Federal Principal Register of the U.S. Patent and Trademark Office is highly desirable. Although a certificate of registration does not confer on its owner any guarantee of ownership of the registered name, it carries some very important procedural rights and advantages.

Once a name has been used in commerce in connection with the sale of a product or the promotion and delivery of services, its registration establishes *prima facie* evidence of ownership. This means that, in a lawsuit against an alleged infringer, the registrant does not have to establish by factual evidence his right to the exclusive use of the name. All he needs to do is enter his certificate of registration into evidence. This dispensation from the presentation of factual evidence may allow the plaintiff to obtain a restraining order or a preliminary injunction in the early phase of the case, without going through the protracted proceedings that might be required to establish this ownership. As was demonstrated in Chapter 5, the name of the game in this type of litigation is to obtain such temporary relief, and cases are often won or lost on the outcome of the preliminary proceedings.

A federal registration may be recorded with the U.S. Customs Service to prevent the entry into this country of unauthorized goods bearing the registered mark. The U.S. Customs Service will readily seize counterfeit merchandise at the port of entry. Without the benefit of the trademark registration, the trademark owner might be obligated to bring a series of lengthy and expensive infringement actions before various courts of law against the importers and distributors of the infringing goods.

Registered marks bring into effect various sections of certain statutes, such as the Trademark Counterfeiting Act, that provide for punitive and other special damage awards, as well as the recovery of attorney's fees and court costs not usually granted at common law.

After five years of registration under the Lanham Act, the mark becomes generally incontestable. It cannot even be challenged as being merely descriptive! Registration thus affords a risky but highly effective way to bootstrap a legally weak name into a very strong position.

A federal registration is a convenient stepping-stone for obtaining registration in practically all industrialized countries under the Paris Convention for the Protection of Industrial Property. In most foreign jurisdictions, the right to the exclusive use of a name is based on the name's registration, instead of its use in commerce, and a Paris Convention priority of up to six months can be claimed from the date of filing of the U.S. application. This filing is the best assurance you can buy against foreign trademark pirates, some of whom are known to survey the U.S. market to spot successful name brands that appear to be good candidates for export. These unscrupulous individuals immediately register those brands in their own name and offer the certificates of registration for sale to the U.S. company at extortionary prices. Jerome Gilson reports the mischievous prank of an American expatriate living in Paris who registered the name EXXON and various combinations of that term, including EXXON PROVENCE (Aix-en-Provence being an old provincial capital and the birthplace of Paul Cezanne), before Standard Oil of New Jersey.

If for some reason a federal registration cannot be obtained, the search report might indicate whether a local state registration is possible. This territorially limited form of registration may provide adequate protection in the case of a trade name or service mark intended for local use only.

The Lanham Act established two separate registers of marks. The Principal Register is reserved for fully qualified names and carries all the procedural rights and advantages already mentioned. The Supplemental Register is accessible to descriptive and other legally defective marks yet capable of acting as indications of origin. The main advantage of an entry on the Supplemental Register is that it carries the same Paris Convention priority rights that attach to a registration on the Principal Register. In interpreting the availability search report, be careful about confusing the two types of registrability.

INTRINSIC VALUE

The last issue to be addressed in an availability search report concerns the market-oriented attributes of the commercial name. The valuation that can be given the name upon the sale of the business or the ability to franchise or merchandise the name separately is something to be concerned about from the outset. This intrinsic character of a name is not only rooted in the name's legal strength and marketing appeal, but it also transcends these qualities to give the name a certain degree of universality and general interest to a large segment of the market. It is what allows the name to be used in connection with the manufacture, promotion, and distribution of vastly different products or services and to invade fields of use unrelated to the initial application of the name.

The most compelling reason yet to consult a practitioner with extensive experience in the area of commercial name protection and exploitation is that such an individual can readily rule out certain types of candidate names without having to conduct a search of any kind. Depending upon the intended use, a name may be disqualified by its generic or descriptive character. It has been reported that over 75 percent of name prospects that are searched are found to be unavailable for the intended use. A judicious preliminary screening by the specialist could, in many cases, avoid the delays and expenses of unnecessary searches. Since, by reason of their positive results, a large majority of "idiot searches" must be repeated for alternative candidates, the professional search may turn out to be more economical and avoid a great deal of frustration or the risk of a costly mistake.

In the case of *Mayo v. Chipala*, Mayo sought the aid of an attorney in incorporating a series of thrift shops under the name RE-SELL-IT. The attorney told Mayo that he did not do name availability searches but that he knew a company that did. That company, a nationally advertised search service, conducted a search and reported that only one other company used the name. The attorney, however, noticed that the service had searched the wrong business class and so informed his client. Mayo, unhappy with this report, fired the attorney and then proceeded to sell his business for $500,000, but under a clause that provided for rescision if it were discovered that RE-SELL-IT was not an exclusive name. When the buyer learned that a chain of thrift stores in Saint Louis was operating under that very name, the price was renegotiated downward to $175,000. Mayo sued the attorney for malpractice but lost. The court decided that the attorney had been fired before the case was over; accordingly, he could not be held liable for the consequences of something he did not have a chance to complete.

This conclusion is somewhat disturbing since the attorney made several gross mistakes in handling the case. First, since he realized that he was not qualified to conduct a search, the attorney should have referred his client to a trademark specialist. Second, the attorney used a searching service whose work product required a legal interpretation that he was not competent to make. Without need of a search, the specialist would have pointed out that the proposed name was merely descriptive, had little intrinsic value, and lacked the legal clout required to support a successful franchise operation. Instead of that valuable advice, Mayo was handed the results of a botched and futile availability search. One can understand his frustration and his resentment, although his hasty reliance on the tainted name cannot be condoned. What's in a name, in a good commercial name? In this case, $325,000. This sum could have paid for a lot of advice from the best practitioners in the field.

Before you adopt any kind of commercial moniker, you should order a thorough search to verify its availability, enforceability, registrability, and intrinsic commercial value. Do not rely on the results of a mechanical searching service, unless you have the expertise to judiciously direct its investigation and evaluate its work product. Engage, instead, the services of a qualified expert, and insist upon a detailed opinion dealing with every one of these four critical issues.

CHAPTER 14

PICKING THE WINNER

This chapter deals with the formulation and application of a rating system for selecting the best commercial name prospect among several qualifying candidates. The rating system is based upon a scale developed for use by professional namesmiths. The model proposed here is only an example. You may elect to modify it by adding factors particularly relevant to your case, or you may decide to design your own grading method. The essential point is that you make a rational approach, taking into account as many as possible of the criteria applicable to the creation of an effective name.

PRELIMINARY SCREENING

The suggested rating system is only effective when applied to qualified commercial names, that is, names that are available and that can legally act as company, product, or service identifiers. You know by now that only distinctive names can fulfill that role and that the only names that are available are those that can be used without creating a likelihood of confusion with any other name already used in commerce.

The problem with availability and distinctiveness is that they are relative concepts that often evade absolute judgment. It has already been demonstrated how a weak name that is already on the market can still be available for application in a slightly different milieu or field of use. GOLDEN STATE, a name particularly popular in California, is used by unrelated parties without any likelihood of confusion in the field of transportation, as GOLDEN STATE AVIATION, GOLDEN STATE FLYING CLUB, GOLDEN STATE CRAFTS, GOLDEN STATE TOURS, GOLDEN STATE TOWING, GOLDEN STATE TRANSPOR-TATION COMPANY, and many more. The name GOLDEN STATE is so trite, so ordinary, that the public does not presume any kind of kinship between the large number of firms operating under this vocable. By contrast, a strong name like JELLI-BEANS can preempt the use of not only same or similar-sounding words, but also other candy names, such as LOLLIPOPS, in connection with the same type of business (skating rink). The distinctive name GREYHOUND, used in connection with bus lines, precludes its use by others in connection with financial services. GREYHOUND is such a well-known service that the court feared that the public would look at an investment service called GREYHOUND as a diversified activity of the famous transportation company.

Distinctiveness and availability are concepts that not only are difficult to pin down, they are also cross-related. The more distinctive the name, the broader is its field of preemption, and vice versa. Since no absolute judgment can be passed in these matters, it would be unwise to eliminate potential name candidates at the outset on the sole ground of prior use or lack of distinctiveness, except in the most extreme cases.

The legal characterizations of commercial names listed in Chapter 5 indicate that names classified as generic and commonly descriptive are totally unprotectible. This type of name should be ruled out of competition in the rating system. Names that are identified during the availability search as similar to a name already in use by competitors for the same purpose must also be disqualified. You may retain as qualifying candidates all other choices and creations, including merely descriptive names and names used by competitors in the same and related fields, but not for exactly the same purpose. This preliminary screening sometimes calls for some difficult judgments. When in doubt, opt for the safest route and rule out the questionable prospects, lest you take the risk of accepting an unqualified name. As explained in the preceding chapter, a competent searcher will weed-out generic and commonly desciptive terms from the outset.

LEGAL STRENGTH

The next step is to grade the candidates according to their degree of legal strength in accordance with the principles discussed in Chapter 5. The simple grid in Table 14–1 incorporates sets of rating coefficients that have been assigned and tested by attorneys specializing in trade name and trademark law. The legal

TABLE 14–1
Legal Criteria Rating Table.

Degree of Originality	Type of Name		Field of Prior Use				Graphic, Phonetic, or Semantic Similarity
	(M) Mark	(T) Trade Name	(n) New	(s) Same	(r) Related	(d) Distant	
Merely Descriptive (U)	1	4	9	1 2 5	2 5 7	3 8 10	Exact (e) Close (c) Partial (p)
Mildly Descriptive (V)	3	4	9	1 2 3	2 3 5	2 7 9	Exact (e) Close (c) Partial (p)
Highly Suggestive (W)	4	5	9	1 1 2	1 3 4	2 5 7	Exact (e) Close (c) Partial (p)
Mildly Suggestive (X)	6	7	10	1 1 2	1 2 3	1 3 6	Exact (e) Close (c) Partial (p)
Fanciful Borowed (Y)	9	9	10	1 1 1	1 2 3	1 2 5	Exact (e) Close (c) Partial (p)
Fanciful Coined (Z)	10	10	10	0 1 1	1 1 2	1 1 4	Exact (e) Close (c) Partial (p)
	Creativity Weight		Availability Factor				

strength of a name candidate is the product of its creativity weight with its availability factor.

The creativity weights are found in the left section of the grid and depend upon the type of name candidate and the degree of originality that went into its creation. They are based on a synthesis of current case law and closely reflect the various degrees of strength that a court could attribute to a commercial name. The creativity weight depends upon whether the name is to be used as a mark (trademark or service mark), in which case the weight is found under column (M), or as a trade name, in which case the weight must be taken from column (T). This specific weighting reflects the different degrees of sensitivity to descriptiveness between the two types of commercial names. Ordinarily, trade names can be slightly more descriptive than trademarks or service marks and still retain the same level of protectibility.

The degrees of originality are listed in the far left-hand column and provide horizontal entries to rows labeled (U) through (Z). The six horizontal rows cover the whole spectrum of originality or distinctiveness, from merely descriptive terms to fancifully coined ones, except for the generic and commonly descriptive types that are disqualified. Thus, the creativity weight assignable to a mildly suggestive corporate name (trade name) is listed at the intersection of column (T) and row (X) as 7. The creativity weight for a fanciful coined name used in connection with a fast-food franchise operation (a service mark) is listed at the intersection of column (M) and row (Z) as 10.

The availability factors in the right-hand section of the grid in Table 14–1 are predicated upon the nature and status of the names as determined during the availability search. These factors are objectively assigned in accordance with the legal criteria used by judges to assess the likelihood of confusion between two names. They have been prudently adjusted for use by laypeople rather than by experienced lawyers to limit the risk of selecting an infringing term. The availability factors depend upon the field of use of the prior name and upon its degree of similarity with the candidate. The possible fields of prior use are spread over three columns, labeled (s) for "same," (r) for "related," and (d) for "distant." The degrees of similarity are presented in each row on three levels, marked (e) for "exact," (c) for "close," and

(p) for "partial." These last three labels define the degree of graphic, phonetic, or semantic similarity between the name candidate and names already in use in the marketplace.

Here are some examples to help you understand what is meant by similarity: PAQ would be treated as an exact phonetical equivalent of PAK, PAC, or PACK. COMPAQ and COMPAL have a close similarity phonetically as well as graphically. Semantically, COLT is similar to PONY, FOCUS is close to TARGET, and LOLLIPOPS is partially equivalent to JELLIBEANS. Courts have found HIBVAX to be the exact equivalent of HIB-IMMUNE and DOGIVA to be closely related to GODIVA.

Returning to the labels at the right-hand top of the chart, the (n) column lists the availability factors corresponding to candidate names that exhibit no sameness or similarity to any other prior commercial designation. The availability factor of a candidate name that is not unique falls under either the (s), (r), or (d) column, depending upon the field in which the prior name is used. GOLDEN STATE AVIATION is in the *same* field of aviation as GOLDEN STATE CRAFTS, and GOLDEN STATE TOURS is in the field of tourism, which is *related* to the field of aviation.

In the worst case, where exactly the same name is already in use in the same general field, the availability factor of the candidate is found under column (s) in one of the subdivisions labeled (e). All of these entries correspond to the whole range of findings derived from the availability search report.

For practice, let us grade a few names that have been encountered earlier in this book.

The legal grade for GOLDEN STATE TOURS as a mark for touring services, in view of the prior use of GOLDEN STATE AVIATION for small aircraft sales, rental, and maintenance services, is the product of its creative weight 9, found in box (M,Y) for a fanciful, borrowed service mark, and the availability factor 1, found in box (Y,r,e), in view of the prior use of the name with exactly the same spelling in a related field. The two names have been treated as exactly similar, without taking into account the descriptive words TOURS and AVIATION. If we were to take those words into account, we would have a creativity weight of 3 in box (M,V) and an availability factor of the same value in box (V,r,c) for a mildly descriptive, closely similar term with a prior use in a related field. Coincidentally, the same grade is obtained in both cases. In spite of this coincidence between the two grading methods, the descriptive tails should ordinarily be ignored and only the first method followed.

The trade name HALLMARK for a construction business, taking into consideration the greeting card company operating under that name, would deserve a creativity weight of 9 from box (T,Y) and an availability factor of 1 from box (Y,d,e) because of the identical term previously used in a field unrelated to the borrowed, fanciful candidate.

The trademark DOGIVA for dog biscuits was selected in spite of the famous GODIVA brand of chocolate candies. That name would get its grade from boxes (M,Z) and (Z,r,c,), as a fanciful, coined mark with a closely similar mark used in a related field, and rate a low 10 in the system.

HANG TEN leads us to boxes (T,Y) and (Y,n)—new, fanciful, borrowed term—and deserves a grade of 90. KODAK (as adopted by George Eastman) would top the scale with a 100 from boxes (T,Z) and (Z,n) as a new, fanciful, coined name. As is apparent, the higher the score, the stronger the name's legal clout.

MARKETING FACTORS

In addition to the legal grade derived by means of the grid system just described, there are other factors that should be taken into consideration when rating name candidates. Of equal importance to the legal criteria are the market-oriented considerations, that is, anything that promotes the named company, product, or service. Those considerations are summarized in Figure 12–5. In that chart, you can find the marketing factors presented from two different angles. Under the column labeled "Effects" are the direct effects resulting from the various semonemic techniques practiced by the name-maker. The listed effects are mirrored in the customer reactions in the next column. We can rate names either by assigning a grade for each listed effect or by assigning a grade for each reaction and then adding the total score. Table 14–2 offers a grading scale for each

TABLE 14–2
Marketing Criteria Rating Table.

Evocation:	0–40 points		Comprehension:	0–50 points
Involvement:	0–30 points		Recollection:	0–30 points
Penetration:	0–20 points		Appeal:	0–20 points
Aesthetics:	0–10 points			
Total:	0–100 points		*Total:*	0–100 points

method. The highest grade that can be achieved in either case is 100. When properly conducted, both types of grading on the same name should be roughly equivalent. Their average is a reliable measure of the market value of the name. Let us examine how this grading can best be accomplished.

Surveys conducted among a specific or a general group of consumers can be very helpful in assessing the value and effectiveness of a commercial name. Care must be taken, however, to ensure that the polled individuals are only asked questions that they are fully competent to answer. Public surveys are particularly helpful for grading a name to determine whether the message that the name is intended to convey is, in fact, perceived by the public; whether the name is easily remembered; and whether the customer finds the name appealing. The survey questionnaire should include only specific questions designed to obtain the individual's spontaneous reactions rather than his value judgments. The following questions would be indicated:

- "What does this word remind you of?" This is a good test of the consumer's comprehension of the intended message and of the pleasant feeling he should experience upon hearing the name.
- "Can you repeat to me all of the following names?" (List five or six names, including the candidate.) This helps you to assess the memorability of the name.

In a survey that seeks to assess the effectiveness of the brand name TOPBRASS for a line of office furniture, such broad inquiries as, "Is TOPBRASS a good name for office furniture?" and "Would you buy a desk sold under the mark TOPBRASS?" are far too complex. They call for expert judgments on several technical issues that the individual may not be qualified to render. A better query would be: "What does the term TOPBRASS suggest to you in connection with a line of office furniture?" If a high percentage of polled subjects answer: "Furniture made with lots of brass parts," the conclusion must be that the message got lost in the translation. If, by contrast, the survey indicates that the name TOPBRASS is perceived as a brand of high-quality equipment for the offices of top corporate executives, you may conclude that the name is right on target and that it also acts as a role model for prospective buyers. Upon hearing it, the consumer sees himself seated behind that TOPBRASS desk like a big executive, just as the young lady who buys COVER GIRL cosmetics imagines herself on the front page of a fashion magazine.

Surveys should only be taken among the targeted class of consumers. For example, the TOPBRASS survey would only be meaningful when conducted among clerical and professional people.

Suppose that you need to determine by a survey whether the name COSMOSTEER or ASTROLEAD is the more appropriate as a new corporate identifier for a major farm equipment manufacturer that has diversified its operation and entered the aerospace and microelectronics market. The *cosmos* and *astro* parts of the names are intended to reflect that broad diversification. The *steer* and *lead* semants are to suggest leadership. The targeted audience is extremely broad—from farmers to avionics engineers and defense contractors. Under these circumstances, two separate surveys—one addressed to farmers, the other to high-technology buyers—might be indicated. The appropriate query would be: "What does the term COSMOSTEER (or ASTROLEAD) suggest to you in connection with farm equipment (or in connection with electronic hardware)?" If either or both types of polled individuals mention any kind of bovine in connection with COSMOSTEER, you may safely conclude that the name would be more appropriate as a brand of manure than as a corporate identifier. If ASTROLEAD elicits too many references to navigational equipment, the term is probably too narrow and fails to reflect the broad diversification of the industrial concern.

The previous examples illustrate the proper use of surveys, whether they are conducted among a large group of consumers, a select panel of executives, or a handful of major customers. The surveys should be limited to testing the spontaneous reactions—comprehension, recollection, or appeal—rather than looking for deliberate answers or educated guesses. When trying to grade a name according to its intended effects—evocation, involvement, penetration, and aesthetics—a popular survey is out of the question. These are issues that must be objectively analyzed by knowledgeable persons. A good student of psychology would be able to decide what kind of image the name would impart in the mind of the targeted buyer and whether that individual would identify with that name. An English major could evaluate the aesthetic quality and penetration of the candidate name. If that kind of expertise is not available, use your best judgment to grade the name yourself. As long as you are consistent in your grading process from name to name, you should have no great difficulty in identifying the most effective of all the name candidates.

The final rating for each name is obtained by adding the legal grade to the marketing grade. As a general rule, very few names exceed a rating of 180 on the 200-point scale. A name that does not score higher than 90 should be rejected. It either lacks commercial value, or worse still, it may constitute a legal time bomb. Any name rated above 150 can be considered an excellent find.

GRADING EXERCISE

Let us assume that you have narrowed your quest for a bank name to three candidates: FORTUNA BANK, SUBURBANK, and TEMPLAR BANK. These names were created according to the semonemic principles and methods expounded earlier in this book, given the following premises: a small commercial bank with six branches in the suburbs of a large Sunbelt city, catering mainly to small business people, shopkeepers, and tradespeople, as well as local professionals, including physicians, dentists, and lawyers.

The availability search has uncovered the following related commercial names:

- FORTUNE, a monthly magazine dealing with business and finances that has a large nationwide audience
- SUNBURST BANK in the same community
- TEENPLAN, a student insurance policy offered by a leading carrier
- PILLARS SECURITIES, an investment brokerage firm in a nearby town

You now proceed with the task of grading the name candidates to make a final selection. The scores are kept in the chart of Table 14–3.

On the legal rating grid, the creativity weight and availability factor for FORTUNA BANK are found in boxes (M,Y) and

TABLE 14–3
Rating Exercise

	Fortuna Bank	Suburbank	Templar Bank
Evocation	30	10	25
Involvement	20	20	25
Penetration	14	11	13
Aesthetics	5	7	5
Total:	69	48	68
Comprehension	35	10	35
Recollection	27	26	20
Appeal	12	12	15
Total:	74	48	70
Average	71.5	48	69
Legal grade	18	20	27
Final score	89.5	68	96

(Y,r,c) as a fanciful, borrowed name with a close equivalent (the FORTUNE publication in a related field). It deserves a grade of 18. SUBURBANK gets its ratings from the (M,Z) and (Z,r,p) boxes as a fanciful, coined name, but with another bank operating in the area under the partially similar-sounding name of SUNBURST BANK. It merits a grade of 20. TEMPLAR BANK, when compared to the insurance policy name of TEENPLAN, leads to boxes (M,Y) and (Y,d,p) as a fanciful, borrowed name having a partially phonetic equivalent in an unrelated field of use. It scores a 45 on the legal strength scale. However, if we compare TEMPLAR BANK to PILLARS SECURITIES, we must go to box (Y,r,p) to find the availability factor because the words PILLARS and TEMPLAR have partially similar phonetic as well as semantic contents. Both words imply stability and strength. Accordingly, the applicable lower grade of 27 must be adopted.

Turning now to the marketing factors, we can give FORTUNA 30 points for evocation by reason of its strong reference to the word *fortune*. For involvement, we will add 20 points, mainly because of the model or goal-setting identification with the class of professionals and other usually ambitious self-employed customers to whom the services are aimed. The fact that FORTUNA is strongly associated with a common word with a relatively strong aural impact calls for a 14 in penetration. Aesthetically, the name has mediocre appeal and does not deserve more than 5 points.

SUBURBANK only refers to the suburbs where the bank is located. Since there is no inspiring connotative message in that word, it deserves no more than a 10 for evocation. Because, however, there is a certain degree of identification between the targeted suburbanites and the name, we give it a 20 in involvement. The fusion technique that highlights the name deserves no more than 11 points for penetration. Its aesthetic appeal rises slightly above the average. Let us grant it a 7 for its balance and alliteration.

TEMPLAR BANK is a name that brings to mind not only the Knights Templars, but also the splendor, solidity, and sacredness of Solomon's temple. This last image is particularly fitting for conveying the strength, security, and formality (some might say solemnity or stuffiness) that characterize banking practices. It merits 25 points for evocation. Many of the targeted customers correspond to a class of individuals who constitute the bulk of the membership of fraternal societies, lodges, and other similar organizations whose rituals draw heavily on mid-Eastern tradition. Most such associations trace their roots to the Crusaders and Knights Templars. In view of this strong identification, we can allow 25 points for involvement. The association with the character of the Knights Templars and the relatively hard-hitting sound of the name deserve a 13 for penetration. For aesthetics, no more than an average 5 can be given.

After totaling the market relevance scores, we find FORTUNA BANK ahead with 69 points, followed by TEMPLAR BANK with 68 points, and only 48 points credited to SUBURBANK.

Let us now suppose that you have conducted a survey to test the comprehensibility, memorability, and general appeal of those three names among the targeted audience. You have asked the pertinent questions to verify that the intended messages have been perceived, that the potential customers have no trouble remembering the candidate names, and to test the targeted audience's aesthetic preferences. Some presumed polling results are tabulated and totaled in the chart in Table 14–3, giving 74 points to FORTUNA BANK, 70 points to TEMPLAR BANK, and 48 points to SUBURBANK. This rating is consistent with the previous analysis. After averaging the analysis and survey scores, and then adding the grades based on legal considerations, we obtain disqualifying grades of 89.5 and 68 for FORTUNA BANK and SUBURBANK, respectively. Only TEMPLAR BANK survives the test with a marginal score of 96.

This was only an exercise using hypothetical facts and circumstances, and no conclusion should be drawn from it as to the relative merits of the commercial names analyzed here. What you must remember is that, with a carefully devised methodology, concurrent candidate names can be rationally weighed according to all relevant legal and marketing considerations to expose the most effective one.

DELIVERY

Once the best name candidate has been selected and its effectiveness confirmed by a survey, a graphic artist should be called to design the logo. As explained in Chapter 12, the artist must be made aware of the commercial message that the name seeks to convey so that his graphic interpretation will support, rather than distract, from the name's semantic impact.

If the name is to be presented to a board of directors or an executive committee whose members did not actively participate in the name-making process, you must be careful to explain the reasoning behind the name choice. Your presentation is sure to clash with preconceived, and often mistaken, ideas in the minds of those directors and executives about the kind of name the company needs. Do not be surprised if your initial disclosure is greeted with expressions of disbelief, shock, and even despair. Ask your audience to keep an open mind until you have had a chance to fully explain the value and merits of the name. Suggest that judgment be reserved until that name sinks into the members' psyches and until they hear all the survey evidence and legal opinions that confirm the name's strength and effectiveness. Think of your creation as a utilitarian work of art—a bridge or a building. The Brooklyn Bridge and the Eiffel Tower were seen by many as ugly monstrosities when first erected. So it often is with commercial names until their aesthetics and utility are fully understood and appreciated.

CHAPTER 15

NAME ACQUISITION AND REGISTRATION

In this country, no one, not even the name's creator, can claim a proprietary right to a commercial name until the name is used in commerce. When the name is used in commerce, an exclusive right to the use of the name vests in the legal entity that actually uses the name, whether the entity is an individual or a company. It follows that the final step in the creation of a new name is the commercial use of that name, since only after such commercial use can the mark be registered.

USE IN COMMERCE

The extent of commercial use required for legal acquisition of a name depends upon the true nature of the commercial name as defined in Chapter 1; that is, whether it is intended as a trade name, a trademark, or a service mark.

A trade name identifies an institution that conducts a commercial activity and that is seen as a legal entity by the state, government agencies, and local administrations. Thus, any dealings with either a public agency, another commercial institution, or the public brings the trade name to life. Putting up a sign that bears the trade name, filing articles of incorporation with the secretary of state, hiring an employee, ordering some goods under the trade name, or even tendering a business card to a prospective customer are enough to establish a trade name and to confer ownership of that name on its first user.

Trademarks and service marks are subject to more stringent standards of use before there can be a claim of exclusive ownership. The exclusive right to a trademark accrues to the person or institution that uses the mark in commerce in connection with the sale or distribution of goods to others. The phrase "in connection with" has been construed to mean in close association with the goods by way of labels or tags applied to the goods or to the goods' containers or by printing directly on the goods or containers. Basically, the trademark must be placed in such a way as to give the prospective buyer a reasonable indication as to the product's source.

Inserting an advertising pamphlet or flyer in the product's container has been found to be insufficient use of the mark. But a retail store display of unmarked merchandise under a sign bearing the mark has been found to constitute a use in connection with the sale of the goods.

The exclusive right to a service mark may be acquired by promoting and rendering services to the public under that mark. Placing a newspaper advertisement for mail-order photographic film-processing services under a distinctive name, coupled with the capability and willingness to perform such services, constitutes adequate use of the name.

Under common law, the scope of the exclusive right to a commercial name in terms of territory and field of use extends only as far as the actual use of the name. Under this theory, the mere display of a trade name or service mark on a storefront only prevents the adoption by another of the same name or mark in the area frequented by the patrons of that store. It does not prevent the use of the same identity by a noncompetitor as long as there is no likelihood of confusion among the public. In most jurisdictions, this situation has been modified by various statutes that provide for countywide or statewide protection of trade names (often called business names or fictitious names) once they are entered in a local or state register. The Lanham Act extends nationwide protection to a mark that is used in a type of commerce regulated by the U.S. Congress (usually interstate commerce or commerce between the United States and a foreign country). Similarly, the commercial field preempted by a mark has been somewhat broadened by the definition of statutory classes under which a name or mark can be registered. For example, a mark registered under the Lanham Act in the "Insurance and Financial Services" classification would not be available to other parties for use in such diverse activities as banking and bookkeeping services. Some state laws, such as those of California, give considerable credit to commercial names first used in other jurisdictions and accord them precedence over domestic but subsequently used names. Antidilution legislation, notably in New York and California, prevents the adoption of a commercial name that is the same or similar to a name already in use (even in the absence of competition or likelihood of confusion), on the theory that the unrelated use of a distinctive name tends to weaken the name's originality and impact.

A broad scope of exclusivity can thus be conferred on a commercial name by early and judicious use of it in various territories and fields of activity, coupled with appropriate registrations at the local, state, and federal levels.

AVOIDING LOSS OF OWNERSHIP

The exclusive right to the use of a commercial name can be lost under four distinct sets of circumstances:

1. By expressed or implied abandonment
2. Through misuse of the name
3. Because of lack of enforcement against infringers
4. When the name has become generic

Since the exclusive right to a distinctive commercial name is acquired by the name's use in commerce, that same right can be lost if the name's owner ceases to use the name. A company may be found to have abandoned a name if it has overtly expressed its intent to do so and has ceased to use it, or if it has stopped using the name for some time without apparent intention to employ it again in the near future. That abandonment may be total or limited to a particular territory or field of use. A company that ceases to operate in a particular area or drops a product line may unintentionally allow another to pick up its trade name or trademark in that area or in connection with that line of product. The only legal barrier to a newcomer's concurrent use of the name in neglected areas or fields of application is the likelihood of confusion that might be created in the mind of the public. A deliberate change of a product name or corporate identity, especially when the change is broadly trumpeted as a publicity stunt, leaves the door wide open to the capture of the discarded identifier by an astute competitor or newcomer who, by adopting the abandoned identifier, could acquire some of the goodwill still associated with it.

A company can also lose its dominion over a commercial name by reason of improper use. Allowing some other entity to independently use a proprietary name not only negates the exclusive right to that name but also constitutes an abuse of public trust. The theory is that the public is entitled to rely upon an established commercial name as a warranty of quality. The customer is therefore exposed to a deception if a new product or service is offered from a new, unproven source under the same label as the old one. Naked licensing—that is, the granting of a trademark or service mark license without provision for quality control by the licensor—may result in forfeiture of the exclusive right to the mark.

Failure to aggressively police the field to protect against others' unauthorized or improper uses of a commercial name destroys the name's exclusive and distinctive status and consequently results in a loss of proprietary right in the name. A legal theory called "latches" prevents a plaintiff, for equitable reasons, from pursuing an infringer after too long a time has elapsed. What constitutes too long a time is subject to judicial interpretation based on factual circumstances.

Finally, ownership of a commercial name may be lost if the name becomes generic—that is, if the name has become the common descriptive name of the goods or services in connection with which it is used. In other words, the name has become a common substantive or a verb. Many once-famous trademarks have turned into such generic nouns as aspirin, cellophane, brassiere, celluloid, kerosene, linoleum, thermos, nylon, and many others whose great success and popularity became the main cause of their downfall.

Attaining the pinnacle of success and popularity is probably the least concern of a fledgling entrepreneur or the manufacturer of a new product. Accordingly, the threat of loss due to the name's becoming generic should not concern the name-maker. However, it is an issue of great importance to the owners of such popular names as XEROX and SANKA, who spend large sums trying to educate the public in the proper use of their monikers. Television commercials for the famous decaffeinated brand of instant coffee repeatedly refer to "SANKA brand coffee" rather than simply SANKA. All of these efforts may not prevent the mark SANKA from eventually becoming the common designation for the decaffeinated coffee product it now identifies; nor may they save XEROX from turning into a predicate or a noun as a result of the too commonly heard request, "Please xerox this document," even though the office copier is a CANON.

The commercial names most likely to succumb to the onset of **genericness** are coined ones that are almost totally fanciful and devoid of any other significance, except for the designation of a new product; to wit: aspirin, linoleum, cellophane. If there is some substance to this observation, then SANKA, which was presumably coined from the French *sans* (meaning "without") and *ka* (for caffeine) may fare better than the nonsensical XEROX. It would also follow that sterile names should be avoided in favor of more expressive ones. This is the only lesson that you, as a namesmith, should draw from these comments about the genericness problem.

MARKINGS AND STATUTORY NOTICES

The initials T.M. may be used next to a trademark (S.M. in the case of a service mark) at any time, even before any registration, to indicate the status of the name and the user's claim to exclusivity. This is particularly recommended if the mark is somewhat descriptive and could be mistaken for a mere definition of the goods or services. To avoid problems of misuse and the danger of the name becoming generic, always print the name in a bolder type than the surrounding text and use it as a distinctive modifier rather than in a denominative sense. A promotional pamphlet for a new computer should not state: "The ENSIGN has 560 kilobytes of memory," but rather: "The ENSIGN brand of computer has 560 kilobytes of memory."

The symbol ® must never be used next to a mark until the mark has been duly registered in one of the federal registers. Such a misuse of the registration symbol has been construed to be a misrepresentation to the public of the legal status of the mark, which may prevent its registration or its later enforcement against imitators. The impressive notice "Registered with the U.S. Patent and Trademark Office" can also be used with increased deterrent effect after the mark has been federally registered.

REGISTRATION

The name of a corporation appears in the articles of incorporation that must be filed with the secretary of state as part of the incorporation procedure. The secretary of state's office usually rejects any corporate identifier that conflicts with the name of an already established domestic corporation or of an out-of-state one that is qualified to do business in the state. To that limited extent, the entry of a corporate name in the state administrative files provides a certain degree of protection against the adoption of a similar name by other corporations.

Fictitious commercial names—that is, trade names of sole proprietorships—and D.B.A.'s or other aliases used by corporations receive the same type of local guarantee through entries in the township, county, or state registers of trade names. Some states have defined by statutes the extent of presumptive protection that each level of registration confers on a trade name. These rights and guarantees are not consistent among jurisdictions and cannot be compared to the valuable procedural advantages that are bestowed on commercial names that are entered as trademarks or service marks in the state or federal registers.

Even though a trademark or service mark does not identify a company as a legal entity (COCA-COLA COMPANY) but as a product (COCA-COLA or COKE brand of sodas) or as a service (COCA-COLA franchises), it is nevertheless a good practice to use part of the trade name (COCA-COLA) as a mark and thus secure for the trade name all of the advantages offered by the registration of the mark. If the list of products or services offered by the business is too varied, seek to qualify the dominant part of the corporate name as a service mark. For example, GENERAL MOTORS qualifies as a service mark of the GENERAL MOTORS CORPORATION in connection with automotive services. Thus, almost every distinctive commercial name can, in one way or another, be registered as a trademark or a service mark to secure the maximum degree of statutory protection.

Comment was made in Chapter 13 about the many advantages that accrue to a mark upon the mark's registration with the U.S. Patent and Trademark Office. Such a registration is the first and mandatory step of a sensible trademark or service mark management program. If such a registration cannot be had readily, or during the pendency of its process, you should also consider registration with one or more states. While a state registration has limited territorial coverage and may not offer the procedural leverage conferred by a federal registration, it nevertheless provides some immediate benefits that can effectively buttress the federal registration once it is granted. Some states grant registrants substantive rights and procedural advantages that go beyond those provided under the federal laws, albeit within their limited territorial jurisdictions. California, for example, with its strong antidilution provisions, its own anticounterfeit act, and liberal damage clauses, attracts close to 15,000 applications for registration of trademarks or service marks each year and issues six times as many certificates of registration as New York, the runner-up state.

The registration of a mark is a procedure that appears deceptively simple. Yet, it can turn into a frustrating quarrel with the registration examiner, or worse, into protracted triangular warfare between the applicant, the U.S. Patent and Trademark Office Trademark Trial and Appeal Board, and a third party opposer. Even an expedient state registration raises some critical issues of trademark or service mark characterization, classification, goods or services description, date of first use, priority claim, and disclaimer that may require professional attention. An applicant for federal registration must face additional issues, such

Int. Cl.: 9

Prior U.S. Cl.: 26

Reg. No. 1,377,962

United States Patent and Trademark Office   Registered Jan. 14, 1986

TRADEMARK
PRINCIPAL REGISTER

BushHawk

OCEAN INSTRUMENTS, INC. (CALIFORNIA
CORPORATION)
5312 BANKS STREET
SAN DIEGO, CA 92110

FOR; SHOULDER-STOCK SCOPE AND
CAMERA MOUNTS, IN CLASS 9 (U.S. CL. 26)

FIRST USE 4-30-1985; IN COMMERCE
4-30-1985.

SER. NO. 543,183, FILED 6-17-1985.

JOHN P. RYNKIEWICS, EXAMINING
ATTORNEY

as choice of register, date of first use in a type of commerce regulated by Congress, concurrent use, membership and certification mark characterization, and label compliance with other Federal statutes, not to mention the complex adversary proceedings of an opposition. In other words, registration of a mark involves practically every aspect of the arcane laws and procedures of trademark practice that are best left to an experienced intellectual property specialist. Do not be influenced by those who claim to have successfully registered a mark without professional assistance. What they have accomplished may be pale compared to what they have missed, and a latent defect in a mark registration can be fatal to the case when one tries some years later to enforce the exclusive use of the mark through litigation.

CONCLUSION

True ease in *naming* comes from art, not chance,
As those move easiest who have learned to dance.
'Tis not enough no harshness gives offense,
The sound must seem an echo of the sense.

Alex Pope (with a twist)

By now, you must certainly accept the initial premise that the art of naming companies and products does not call for flashes of creativity or fortuitous discoveries, but for organization, hard work, and a good understanding of the concept of distinctiveness, which lends marketing effectiveness and legal clout to a name. You have learned to look at commercial identifiers as subtle but cogent advertisements, effective positioners, protectors, and valuable commodities. You know how to draw the blueprints for the creation of powerful names, using all of the pertinent information that can be gathered, not only about the goods, business, or services to be named, but also about the all-important customer. You appreciate the wealth and flexibility of the English idiom and can manipulate its semantic wheels and cogs to coin the most mellifluous, motivating, and memorable monikers, keeping in mind the poet's monition quoted above.

In spite of this, you may decide, after all, that semonemics is not your cup of tea or that you are too busy an entrepreneur or corporate executive to tinker with prefixes, suffixes, semants, and phonemes. In fact, you may prefer to turn the task of naming your new company or creation over to someone else. Too bad you will miss the fun, but all is not lost, and much positive fallout remains. Your reading of this book will have taught you enough to be able to recognize and select a qualified name-crafter, to know how to work harmoniously with him, and to get the most out of his labor.

During the last decade, there has emerged a breed of self-appointed name-consultants who have exacted exorbitant fees from unwary executives for the creation of shallow and sometimes troublesome corporate and product identifiers. You should know how to spot these amateurs; their cut-and-try approach to name-coining is unsystematic, and they hide their ignorance of the basic principles of semonemics behind vague claims of creativity. Further, these magicians show little concern for the possible legal or commercial repercussions of what they pull out of their hats. They may have been lucky enough once or twice to stumble upon a real gem of a name, but remember that a blind pig can sometimes unearth truffles, even though he may not have realized he was in the oak forest, where truffles are always found. What you need, instead, is a naming service with a systematic approach that takes into account the three P's—promotion, protection and profit; one that stands behind its work with a guarantee of market strength and legal validity. You need a partner in the naming process who shares your vision of a name that will immediately catapult your product or company to a prominent and secure posititon.

LEGAL REFERENCES

Preface

CHOICE: *Aetna Health Care Systems, Inc. v. Health Care Choice, Inc.,* 231 USPQ 614, (ND Okla. 1986).

Chapter 1

First California Trademark Statute: Cal. Stats. 1861, Chapter 478.

Trade name: 15 USC 1127, *American Steel Founderies v. Robertson,* 269 US 372, 46 S. Ct. 160 (1926).

Trademark: 15 USC 1127, Restatement 2d Torts 175, *McLean v. Fleming,* 96 US 245 (S. Ct. 1877).

Service mark: 15 USC 1053, 1127, *Boston Professional Hockey Association, Inc. v. Dallas Cap & Emblem Manufacturing, Inc.,* 510 F2d 1004, 185 USPQ 364 (5th Cir.), cert. denied 423 US 868 (1975).

SUPER GLUE: *Loctite Corporation et al. v. National Starch and Chemical Corporation et al.,* 516 F. Supp. 190, 211 USPQ 237.

READER: *Chicago Reader, Inc. v. Metro College Publishing Company,* 711 F2d 801, 222 USPQ 782 (7th Cir. 1983).

LITE: *Miller Brewing Company v. G. Heileman Brewing Company,* 561 F2d 75, 195 USPQ 281, cert. denied 434 US 1025.

WINDSURFER: *Windsurfing International, Inc. et al. v. Fred Osterman GmbH et al.,* 613 F2d 933, 227 USPQ 927 (1985).

SAFARILAND: *Abercrombie & Fitch Company v. Hunting World, Inc.,* 537 F2d 4, 189 USPQ 759 (2d Cir. 1976).

BUILDERS EMPORIUM: *Builders Emporium, Limited v. Vornado, Inc. et al.,* 201 USPQ 935 (N.Y. S. Ct. 1978).

Priority: see also *Exxon Corporation v. Humble Exploration Company, Inc.,* 524 F. Supp. 450, 465 USPQ 451 (ND Texas 1981), aff'd in part, rev'd and remanded in part 695 F2d 96, 217 USPQ 1200, reh'g denied 701 F2d 173 (5th Cir. 1983).

COMPUTERSTORE: In re Computer Store, Inc., 211 USPQ 72 (TTAB 1981).

Chapter 2

Restraining order and seizure of counterfeit goods: Trademark Counterfeiting Act, 18 USC 2320.

U.S. Customs: Customs Regulations, 19 CFR Part 133.

Taxation of proceeds from name transfer: Rev. Rul. 55–694, 65–261.

Chapter 3

Capital gain deduction: I.R.C. 1202(a), 1986 Act 301 (a).

TAYLOR: *Taylor Wine Company, Inc. v. Bully Hill Vineyards, Inc.,* 569 F2d 731, 196 USPQ 593, see also 201 USPQ 65 (2d Cir. 1978).

Lanham Act: Chapter 22 of Title 15 of U.S. Code enacted July 5, 1946, 60 Stat 427, Public Law 489, 59th Congress, Chapter 540.

LITE: *Miller Brewing Company v. G. Heileman Brewing Company,* 561 F2d 75, 195 USPQ 281 (7th Cir. 1977), cert. denied 434 US 1025 (1978). *Miller Brewing Company v. Falstaff Brewing Corporation,* 655 F2d 125, 211 USPQ 665 (1st Cir. 1981). *Miller Brewing Company v. Rainier Brewing Company,* Civ. Act. No C 77–519V (WD Wash. 1980 unreported). *Miller Brewing Company v. Jos. Schlitz Brewing Company,* 605 F2d 990, 203 USPQ 642 (7th Cir. 1979).

COMPUTER STORE: Chapter 1 supra.

APPLE: *Apple Computer, Inc. v. Formula International, Inc.,* 725 F2d 521, 221 USPQ 762 (9th Cir. 1984).

COMPUTERLAND: *ComputerLand Corporation v. Microland Computer Corporation,* 586 F2d 22, 224 USPQ 866 (ND Calif. 1984).

BUILDERS EMPORIUM: Chapter 1 supra.

Likelihood of confusion: *WSM, Inc. v. Hilton,* 724 F2d 1320, 1329, 221 USPQ 410, 417 (8th Cir. 1984).

TENDER VITTLES: *Ralston Purina Company v. Thomas J. Lipton, Inc. et al.,* 341 F Supp 129, 173 USPQ 820 (SDNY 1972).

Chapter 4

GREYHOUND: *Greyhound Corporation v. Greyhound Securities, Inc.,* 26 Misc. 2d 303 (N.Y. S. Ct. 1960).

JELLIBEANS: *Jellibeans, Inc. v. Skating Clubs of Georgia, Inc.,* 716 F2d 833, 222 USPQ 10 (11th Cir. 1983).

Chapter 5

Generic names: *Singer Manufacturing Company v. June Manufacturing Company,* 163 US 169, 16 S. Ct. 1002 (1896).

AIR-SHUTTLE: *Eastern Air Lines, Inc. v. New York Air Lines, Inc.,* 559 Fed. Supp. 1270, 218 USPQ 71 (SDNY 1983).

LITE: Chapter 3 supra.

CONSUMER ELECTRONICS: *CES Publishing Corporation v. St. Regis Publications, Inc.,* 531 F2d 11, 188 USPQ 612 (2d Cir. 1975).

DIAL-A-RIDE: *Urban Mass Transportation Administration v. Ford Motor Company,* 184 USPQ 565 (TTAB 1974).

READER: Chapter 1 supra.

SURGICENTERS: *Surgicenters of America, Inc. v. Medical Dental Surgeries Company,* 601 F2d 1011, 202 USPQ 401 (9th Cir. 1979).

SAFARI: *Abercrombie & Fitch Company v. Hunting World, Inc.,* Chapter 1 supra.

COMPUTERLAND: Chapter 3 supra.

FISH-FRI and CHICK-FRI: *Zatarains, Inc. v. Oak Grove Smokehouse, Inc. et al.,* 698 F2d 786, 217 USPQ 988 (5th Cir. 1983).

PARROT JUNGLE: *Parrot Jungle, Inc. v. Parrot Jungle, Inc. et al.,* 512 F. Supp. 266, 213 USPQ 49 (SDNY 1981).

TELEMED: *Telemed Corporation v. Tel-Med Inc.,* 588 F2d 213, 200 USPQ 427 (7th Cir. 1978).

VISION CENTER: *Vision Center v. Opticks,* 596 F2d 111, 202 USPQ 333 (5th Cir. 1979), cert. denied 444 US 1016 (1980).

CITIBANK: *Citibank N.A. v. Citibanc Group, Inc. et al.,* 215 USPQ 884 (ND Ala. 1982).

OLD HEARTH: *Boston Bakery, Inc. v. Roland Industries, Inc.,* 216 USPQ 799 (TTAB 1982).

UNDERNEATH IT ALL: *Maidenform, Inc. v. Munsingwear, Inc.,* 195 USPQ 297 (SDNY 1977).

ULTRASUEDE: *Spring Mills, Inc. v. Ultracashmere House, Limited,* 724 F2d 352, 221 USPQ 577 (2d Cir. 1983), 532 F. Supp. 1203, 215 USPQ 1057.

OILEX: *Exxon Corporation v. Xoil Energy Resources, Inc. et al.,* 552 F. Supp. 1008, 216 USPQ 634.

REJUVIA: *Del Laboratories, Inc. v. Allegheny Pharmaceutical Corporation,* 516 F. Supp. 777, 215 USPQ 421 (SDNY 1981).

SLICKCRAFT: AMF, Inc. v. Sleekcrafts Boats, 599 F2d 341, 204 USPQ 808 (9th Cir. 1979).

VISA: *VISA International Service Association v. VISA Hotel Group, Inc. et al.,* 561 F. Supp. 984, 218 USPQ 261 (DC Nev. 1983).

JELLIBEANS: Chapter 4 supra.

KODAK: Ex parte Galter, 96 USPQ 216 (P.O. Exam. in Chief 1953).

GREYHOUND: Chapter 4 supra.

HALLMARK: *Hallmark Cards, Inc. v. Hallmark Dodge, Inc.,* 229, USPQ 882 (WD Mo. 1986).

SUPER-GLUE: Chapter 1 supra.

LITE: Chapter 3 supra.

Secondary meaning: *G & C Merriam Company v. Saalfield,* 198 F 369 (6th Cir. 1912) aff'd and modif'd sub nom, *Saafield Publishing Company v. G & C Merriam Company,* 238 F 1 (6th Cir.), cert. denied 243 US 651 (1917).

Fair use: 15 USC 1115b (4).

Chapter 8

LITE: Chapter 3 supra.

Chapter 9

CORNUCOPIA: *Cornucopia, Inc. v. Wagman et al.,* 229 USPQ 908 (Missouri Court of Appeals 1986).

GARBAGE PAIL KIDS: *Original Appalachian Artworks, Inc. v. Topps Chewing Gum, Inc.,* 231 USPQ 850 (ND Ga. 1986).

HERE'S JOHNNY: *Carson et al. v. Here's Johnny Portable Toilet, Inc.,* 698 F2d 831, 218 USPQ 1 (6th Cir. 1983).

Chapter 10

TAS-TEE DRESSING: Henri's Food Products Company, Inc. v. Tasty Snacks, Inc., 231 USPQ 481 (DC EWis. 1986), rev'd and rem'd. . .F2d. . ., 2 USPQ2d 1856 (7th Cir. 1987).

B-WEAR: *Banff, Limited v. Federated Department Stores et al.*, 638 F. Supp. 652, 231 USPQ 55 (SDNY 1986).

SEYCOS: *Seiko Kabushiki Kaisha Hattori Tokeiten v. Scuotto*, 228 USPQ 461 (TTAB 1985).

WUV'S: *Wuv's International, Inc. v. Love's Enterprises, Inc.*, 208 USPQ 736 (DC Colorado).

Chapter 12

Pizza men design: *Pizza Inn, Inc. v. Russo*, 221 USPQ 281 (TTAB 1983).

Eight ball: In re Eight Ball, Inc., 217 USPQ 1183 (TTAB 1983).

United Distributors, Inc.: In re United Distributors, Inc., 238 USPQ 228 (TTAB 1986).

Chapter 13

First use in commerce: *Exxon Corporation v. Humble Exploration Company, Inc.*, 524 F. Supp. 450, 465 USPQ 451 (ND Tex. 1981), aff'd in part, rev'd and rem'd in part 695 F2d 96, 217 USPQ 1200 reh'g denied, 701 F2d 173 (5th Cir. 1983).

Lanham Act: Chapter 3 supra.

Foreign use of name: *American Petrofina, Inc. v. Petrofina of California, Inc.*, 189 USPQ 67 (CD Calif. 1975), aff'd 596 F2d 896, 202 USPQ 354 (9th Cir. 1979).

California law: Business and Professions Code Section 14417.

Federal Trademark Act: Lanham Act, Chapter 3 supra.

California Trademark Act: Business and Professions Code Section 14200 et seq.

California Fictitious Business Name Act: Business and Professions Code Section 14400 et seq.

CHOICE: *Aetna Health Care Systems, Inc. v. Health Care Choice, Inc.*, *Pref. supra.*

Abandonment: 15 USC 1052 (d), 1127, *Saxlehner v. Eisner & Mendelson Company,* 179 US 19, 21 S. Ct. 7 (1900).

CONCORD: *Champion Home Builders Company v. American Motors Corporation,* 197 USPQ 333 (ED Mich. 1978).

DOMINO'S PIZZA: *Amstar Corporation v. Domino's Pizza, Inc.,* 615 F2d 252, 205 USPQ 969 (5th Cir. 1980), cert. denied 449 US 899, 208 USPQ 464 (1980).

SURE: *Procter & Gamble v. Johnson & Johnson, Inc.,* 485 F. Supp. 1185, 205 USPQ 697 (SDNY 1979); see also *Carter Wallace, Inc. v. Procter & Gamble Company,* 434 F2d 794, 167 USPQ 713 (9th Cir. 1970).

JELLIBEANS: Chapter 4 supra.

Opposition: 15 USC 1063.

Registered marks: 15 USC 1051.

Prima facie evidence of ownership: 15 USC 1057 (b).

U.S. Customs: Customs Regulations, 19 CFR Part 133.

Other statutes: Trademark Counterfeit Act 18 USC 2320.

Incontestability: 15 USC 1065, *Park 'N Fly, Inc. v. Dollar Park & Fly, Inc.,* 469 US 189, 105 S. Ct. 658, 224 USPQ 327 (1985).

Paris Convention: Convention for the Protection of Industrial Property (1883).

Supplemental Register: 15 USC 1091–1096, In re Municipal Market Data, Inc., 229 USPQ 472 (TTAB 1986).

RE-SELL-IT: *Mayo v. Chipala,* Vol. 28 PTCJ 306, (11th Cir. 6/9/84 unreported).

Chapter 14

JELLIBEANS: Chapter 4 supra.

GREYHOUND: Chapter 4 supra.

HIBVAX: *American Cyanamid Corporation v. Connaught Laboratories, Inc.,* 800 F2d 306, 231 USPQ 126 (7th Cir. 1986).

DOGIVA: *Grey v. Campbell Soup Company,* 231 USPQ 562 (CD Calif. 1986).

HALLMARK: Chapter 5 supra.

Chapter 15

Use in commerce: *Turner v. HMH Publishing Company,* 380 F2d 224, 228, 154 USPQ 330, 332 (5th Cir.) cert. denied 389 US 1006, 88 S. Ct. 566, 156 USPQ 720 (1967).

Use in other jurisdictions: *American Petrofina, Inc. v. Petrofina of California, Inc.,*189 USPQ 67 (CD Calif. 1975) aff'd 596 F2d 896, 202 USPQ 354 (9th Cir. 1979).

Antidilution: California Business & Professions Code 14330, Illinois Revised Statutes Chapter 140 S 22 (1971), Maine Rev. Stat. Ann. Tit 10, S 1530, Massachusetts General Business Law Annotated Chapter 110, S 7A (1958), Missouri Revised Statutes S 417.061, New York General Business Law 368–d (1968), and others.

Abandonment: Chapter 13 supra.

Naked licensing: *Dawn Donut Company v. Hart's Food Stores, Inc.,* 267 F2d 358, 121 USPQ 430 (2d Cir. 1959).

Genericness: *Bayer Company v. United Drug Company,* 272 Fed 505 (aspirin); *Du Pont Cellophane Company v. Waxed Products Company,* 85 F2d 75 (2d Cir. 1936) (cellophane); *Celluloid Manufacturing Company v. Cellonite Manufacturing Company,* 32 Fed 94 (D N.J. 1887) (celluloid); *Linoleum Manufacturing Company v. Nairn,* L.R. 7 Ch. Div. 834 (1878) (linoleum); *American Thermos Products Company v. Aladdin Industries, Inc.,* 207 F. Supp. 9 (D Conn. 1962) aff'd, *King-Seeley Thermos Company v. Aladdin Industries, Inc.,* 321 F2d 577 (2d Cir. 1963) mod. denied, 289 F. Supp. 155 (D Conn. 1968) (thermos). For test of, see *H. Marvin Ginn Corporation v. International Association of Fire Chiefs,* 782 F2d 987, 222 USPQ 528 (CFAC 1986).

Misuse of ® symbol: *Fox-Stanley Products, Inc. v. Otaguro,* 339 F. Supp. 1293, 174 USPQ 257 (D Mass. 1972); *Four Roses Products Company v. Small Grain Distilling & Drug Company,* 29 F2d 959 (DC Cir. 1928).

Registration: 15 USC 1051–1113.

California Trademark Statute: Business & Profession Code. Antidilution: Section 14330; anticounterfeit: Section 14436; damage clauses: Sections 14340, 14438.

Opposition: 15 USC 1063.

Membership marks: Also called collective marks, 15USC 1054, 1127, *Huber Baking Company v. Strochman Brothers Company,* 252 F2d 945, 116 USPQ 348 (2d Cir.), cert. denied 358 US 829 (1958).

Certification marks: *Schroder v. Lotito,* 577 F. Supp. 708, 221 USPQ 812 (DCRI 1983) aff'd 747 F2d 801, 224 USPQ 97 (1st Cir. 1984).

Corporate names: *Hulburt Oil & Grease Company v. Hulburt Oil & Grease Company,* 371 F2d 251, 152 USPQ 87 (7th Cir. 1966), cert. denied 386 US 1032 (1967).

GLOSSARY OF
TECHNICAL TERMS

acronym   A name created by joining together the first letters of the words of a descriptive phrase, such as NASA from National Aeronautics and Space Administration.

alliteration   The use of the same sound or syllable in succession, as in COCA-COLA.

allusion   Also called evocative reference. The selection as a name of an existing word or phrase that designates a generally known person, fact, or object, such as the mountain name SHASTA for a brand of soft drinks.

analogy   A name-coining technique in which a name is formed in imitation of an existing word; for example, ICE CAPADE by analogy to *escapade*.

answer   A formal pleading filed by a defendant in response to a complaint.

clipping   Also called retrogressive or back formation. The creation of a new name by cutting away the beginning or the end of a word; for example, AUTOMAT.

complaint   The pleading filed by a plaintiff in a lawsuit asserting a claim against one or more defendants.

composition   A name-coining technique whereby several existing words are joined together, as in RAINBIRD.

cross-complaint   A pleading filed by a defendant in a lawsuit asserting a claim against the plaintiff.

D.B.A.   Acronym for "doing business as."

demurrer   A form of legal pleading challenging the form or content of a complaint.

deposition   A legal procedure during which statements made under oath by a party or witness to a lawsuit are taken down or recorded for use as evidence.

determinance   The degree of influence over the customer's choice attributed to a particular feature of the product or company.

discovery   In a lawsuit, the procedure that allows a party to obtain information about the opponent's case by means of interrogatories, requests for documents, requests for admissions, and depositions of parties and witnesses.

emphasis   The various elements of an advertisement that are directed to the senses rather than to the intellect of the customer.

engram   The effect that the sight or sound of a name produces on the psyche.

eponym   The name of one or more individuals used to designate his or their creation; for example, DOW-JONES Index.

etymology   The root and development of a word.

ex parte   Applies to a legal proceeding involving only one litigant without participation of the opponent.

fair use   The use in good faith of a competitor's descriptive commercial name to describe the nature of one's own goods or services.

federal registers   Registers established under the Lanham Act to record marks used in interstate commerce and other forms of commerce regulated by the U.S. Congress.

franchise   A type of license agreement under which a franchisee is authorized, for a fee, to conduct a business under the commercial name of a franchisor and according to specified methods of operation and quality control.

fusion   A form of composition in which letters or syllables common to two component words are merged together, as in SUBURBANK.

genericness   The character of a name that is no more than the common descriptive term for the named product or service.

glide   In phonetics, the letter whose pronounciation requires a slight shift of sound, such as the *y* in *yes*. Also called a semivowel.

handle   A colloquial synonym for *name*.

homonym   Word that sounds like another but has a different meaning; for example, *pear* and *pair*.

ideophones* or **ideophonemes**   Suggestive letters or combinations thereof used in the coining of a commercial name.

---

*Neologism

idiot search   Name availability search conducted manually or by computer looking for graphic or phonetic equivalents of a name candidate without taking into account the pertinent legal criteria.

injunction   A judicial order forbidding one party from doing something. An injunction may be temporary, pending further proceedings, or permanent, as part of a final decree or judgment.

intellectual property   Products of the mind, such as inventions, works of authorship (including artistic creations), accumulated goodwill, and proprietary rights to the above under patent, copyright, trademark, and trade secret laws.

interrogatories   Written questionnaire submitted by one party to a lawsuit to another party to be answered under oath.

jingle   A musical advertisement.

Lanham Act   A Federal statute regarding trademarks and other designations of origin.

license   A contractual arrangement under which a party is given permission to use the proprietary right of another, such as the other's commercial name in exchange for a fee or royalties.

merchandising   A type of license for the use of a name or other proprietary matter in connection with the sale of a variety of goods.

metonymy   The designation of something by the name of a closely related object or concept; for example, as when "the Kremlin" is used in lieu of "the government of the USSR."

moniker or **monicker**   A name (without the disparaging sense ascribed to that word in the British Isles).

morpheme   Fragment of a word that fulfills a grammatical or semantic function.

motion   A request addressed to the court by one party in a lawsuit.

onomatope   A word whose pronunciation imitates the sound made by what that word designates; for example, *jingle, howl, splash.*

onomatopoeia   The use of onomatopes.

orthography   Correct spelling of a word.

patronym   A family name.

phoneme   A particular sound found in a language, like the sound represented by the letters *sh* in *shale* and *shirt.*

Provençal   Also called Langue d'Oc or Occitan. The Romance language of what is now southern France, spoken and spread throughout medieval Europe by the troubadours.

restraining order A preventive injunction.

secondary meaning The identifying character acquired by a descriptive word or phrase as a result of long and exclusive use as a commercial name by a single business concern.

semant* Expressive word fragment.

semantation* The combination of semants taken from various words to form a new expressive name.

semantics A branch of linguistics concerned with the meanings of various forms of speech.

semonemics* The art of creating commercial names to identify companies, products, or services.

service mark The commercial name used by a company in promoting and rendering services to the public; for example, HOLIDAY INN.

summary judgment A court decision based on legal principles and/ or facts already admitted or readily ascertainable by the judge without trial.

sympiptism* The synergistic blending, in a commercial name, of a highly evocative sound with a corresponding image, such as the combination of onomatopoeia and symbolism, to accentuate the impression created by the name.

tacking Also called derivation. The coining of a name by attachment of a prefix or a suffix to a root word.

trademark An identification affixed to goods placed in commerce as an indication of origin. A trademark can be a symbol, a design, or a commercial name, such as KODAK.

trade name The legal name of a business entity; for example, EASTMAN KODAK COMPANY, HOLIDAY INNS OF AMERICA, INC.

vocable Synonym for *name*.

---

*Neologism

BIBLIOGRAPHY

Alibert, Lois. *Gramatica Occitana*. Montpellier, France: Centre d' Estudis Occitans, 1976.

Diamond, Sidney A. *Trademark Problems and How to Avoid Them.* Chicago: Crain Communications, 1973.

Gilson, Jerome. *Trademark Protection and Practice*. New York: Matthew Bender, 1986.

Mencken, H.L. *The American Language*. New York: Alfred A. Knopf, 1985.

Oathout, John D. *Trademarks*. New York: Charles Scribner, 1981.

Ogilvy, David. *Ogilvy on Advertising*. New York: Crown Publishing, 1983.

Pei, Mario. *The Story of Language*. Philadelphia: J.B. Lippincott, 1985.

Robicheaux, Robert A., William M. Pride, and O.C. Ferrell. *Marketing, Contemporary Dimensions*. 2d ed. Boston: Houghton Mifflin, 1980.

U.S. Trademark Association. *Trademark Management*. New York: Clark Boardman Corporation,

INDEX

INDEX

A

Abandonment 113, 136, 137
ABLE-DOE 22
ACAPULCO POOLS 77
ACETAMINOPHEN 57
Acquisition 134–138
Acronym 29, **Glossary**
ACURA 60
ADAPT-A-SWITCH 84
ADAZINE 95
Adams Eddie 71
ADJUSTA-POISE 84
ADJUSTASTROKE 83, 84
Advertising fundamentals 68–70
ADVIL 57
Aesthetic quality 35, 80, 108–110,
　　129, 131
Aetna Health Care System, Inc.
　　Preface, 112
Affinity with buyer 38, 51, 65 *see*
　　also Personal Involvement
AFFORDABLE PLUMBING 23
AIM 59
AIR-SHUTTLE 39
Alias 62, 76
ALLEGIS 60
ALLEREST 98
Alliteration 79, 131, **Glossary**

Allusion 13, 76, 77, 81, 91, 99, 109,
　　Glossary
ALPO 29
AMBERLITE 97
ANACIN 95
Analogy 83, 87, 88, 91, 109,
　　Glossary
Anglo-Saxon languages 94–97
Animal names 75
Answer 42, **Glossary**
Anti-dilution statutes 136, 140
ANTIPHRINE 95
ANTIQUAX 109
APPLE **Preface**, 27, 29, 99
Arbitrary names *see* Fanciful names
ARONDE 75
ARPEGGIO 59
ASPENCADE 88, 91, 95, 109
ASPIRIN, 88, 137, 138
ASTRALLIANCE 85
ASTROLEAD 128
Attorneys 28, 49, 112, 114, 117–120,
　　141
Aural impact 78, 82, 101, 131
AUTOMAT 86, 88, 95, 109
Availability factor 124–126, 130,
　　131
Availability search 28, 111–120, 122
Aztec language 64

B

Back formation *see* Clipping
BACKSEAT SALLY 80
BAKELITE 95
Balance *see* Symmetry
BANANA REPUBLIC 80
B.B.C. 98
BEE WEAR 87
BENJAMIN FRANKLIN POSTAL
    CENTER 77
BIOCHEM 95
BIOVEST 30
BLOODHOUND 33
Borge, Victor 87
BRAHMA 75
Brainstorming **Preface**
BRANDYWINE 77
Brassiere 137
BRICK WAREHOUSE (The) 18
BUILDERS EMPORIUM 11, 27
BUSHHAWK 82, 84, 105, 141
B WEAR 87

C

CABBAGE PATCH 81
Cadence *see* Rhythm
CAESARS PALACE 77
CALIBAKER 91
CAMARGUE 75
CAMELOT 30
CANON 138
Capp, Al 7
CARAVAN 86
CARESS 9
CARPETMASTER 100
CARPETMATE 100
Carroll, Lewis 88
Carson, Johnny 81
CASCADE 72, 79, 99
CASUALETS 95

CELEBRITY 76
CELICA 100
Cellophane 137, 138
Celluloid 137
Certificate of registration 116, 140
Cezanne, Paul 117
CHAIN OF COMMAND 65, 80, 91,
    109
CHAMP 24, 69
CHAPULIN 64, 67, 77, 109
Characters 106, 109
CHARMIN 9
Chaucer, Geoffrey 61
CHEETAH 75
CHERACOL 98
CHEVELLE 5
CHICK-FRI 40
CHLOR-TRIMETON 96, 98
CHOICE **Preface**, 111
CHUCK WAGON 29, 59, 71
CITIBANK 40
Clearance *see* Availability search
Clipping 85, 86, 109, **Glossary**
COCA-COLA 25, 78, 79, 109, 139,
    140
Coca-Cola Co. 25, 139
CODAC 87
COKE 25, 139
Colloquialisms 98
COLT 125
Combination 88
Commercial message 10, 49–53, 56,
    57, 66–70
Common English 58, 59, 81, 102
Common law 111, 112, 117
Commonly descriptive names 87,
    122, 124
COMPAL 95, 125
COMPAQ 125
Complaint 42, **Glossary**
Composition 83, 109, **Glossary**
COMPUTER DATA COMPANY 27

COMPUTERLAND 26, 27, 40
COMPUTER MART 26
COMPUTER MERCHANT 26, 39
COMPUTER STORE 11, 26
CONCORD 115
CONDORMINIUM 88
CON EDISON 30
Confiscation *see* Seizure
Consolidated Foods **Preface**, 18, 54
CONSOLIDATED PLUMBING 23
CONSUMER ELECTRONICS 39
CONTAC 57
Contests to find a name **Preface**, 3
CONTROL DATA CORPORATION 27
Convention priority 117, 118
Coors (Joseph) Brewing Co. 26
Copying *see* infringement
CORDIA 100
CORNUCOPIA 76
COROLLA 100
Corporate names 5, 112, 124, 139
CORVETTE 5, 86
COSMOSTEER 128
COUGAR 7, 75, 91, 109
Counterfeiting 29, 117
COVER GIRL 76, 109, 128
CRAFTSMAN 76
Creativity weight 123, 130
CRESSIDA 60, 61, 100
Cross-complaint 42, **Glossary**
CRUISE 58
CUISINART 76
Customs *see* U.S. Customs
CUTEX 100

D

DATA GENERAL CORPORATION 27
DAY AND NIGHT PLUMBERS 23

D.B.A. 112, 139, **Glossary**
Definitions 20, 23, 75
Demurrer 42, **Glossary**
Deposition 42, **Glossary**
DERMA LA DOUCHE 80
Derivation 83, 85
Descriptive names 23, 26, 32, 39, 40, 43–45, 69, 76, 86, 98, 118, 119, 138
Design 101–106
Determinance 67, **Glossary**
DIAGUIDE 95, 109
DIAL-A-LITE 84
DIAL-A-RIDE 40
DIGITAL CONTROL CORPORATION 27
DIGITAL EQUIPMENT CORPORATION 27
DIPLOMAT 58
Discovery 42, **Glossary**
Disparagement of a name 42
Distinctiveness 5, 23, 35, 37, 45, 80, 84, 87, 99, 103, 113, 115, 121, 122, 124, 143
DOGIVA 125, 126
DOMINO 115
DOMINO'S PIZZA 115
DOM PERIGNON 79
DOVE 71
DUTCH BOY 107

E

Eastman, George 36, 126
Eastman Kodak Co. 36, 41
Eight Ball, Inc. 103, 104
Emphasis 68, 69, **Glossary**
EMPIRIN 88
Enforceability 35, 41–43, 49, 115
Engram 5, 36, 78, 101, **Glossary**
ENSIGN 139

Eponyms 22, **Glossary**
ERCEFURYL 57
ERNIE'S SALON 13
ERYTHROMYCIN 58
Etruscan language 94
Etymological roots 9, 83, 96, 101
Etymology 81, 93, **Glossary**
Evocation 110, 129, 131, 132
Evocative reference 76, 84, 89, 131
EXIDOL 95
Ex parte order 42, **Glossary**
EXXON 23, 82, 91, 117

F

Fair use 45, **Glossasry**
Falstaff Brewing Corporation 25
Family names *see* Patronyms
Family of names 99
Fanciful names 39, 40, 124
FANTA 86
FASHIONETTE 85, 95
Federal registers 79, 80, 113, 116,
    139, **Glossary**
Federal Trademark Act *see* Lanham
    Act
Fictitious names 111, 135, 139
Field of use 41, 57, 113, 124, 136
FIREHAWK 75
FISH-FRI 40
FLEET FINANCIAL GROUP 18
FLEURS DE ROCAILLE 75
Flora 75
Fluidity 80, 109
FOCUS 59, 98, 125
FOLIES BERGERES 102
Ford, Henry 36
Foreign languages 30, 56
Foreign market 30, 31, 56
Foreign registration 117
FORMICA **Preface**, 14, 24, 96
FORTUNA BANK 129–132

FORTUNE 130
Franchise 15, 16, 118, 139,
    Glossary
French language 30, 60, 79, 94–96,
    138
FRUIT OF THE LOOM 79, 109
FUNDERWEAR 80
FUNDERWRITER 85
FURNISHING 2000 18
Fusion 84, 91, 109, 131, **Glossary**

G

Gaelic words 79
GARBAGE PAIL KIDS 81
GATORADE 95
General Electric 107
GENERAL MOTORS 140
GENERAL MOTORS CORPORA-
    TION 5, 140
Generic design 103–106
Generic terms 24, 26, 32, 39, 44, 86,
    118, 122, 124, 137
Genericness 137, 138, **Glossary**
Gilson, Jerome 117, **Bibliography**
Glide 91, **Glossary**
GODIVA 125, 126
GOLDEN STATE 121, 122
GOLDEN STATE AVIATION 122,
    125
GOLDEN STATE CRAFTS 122, 125
GOLDEN STATE FLYING CLUB
    122
GOLDEN STATE TOURS 122, 125
GOLDEN STATE TOWING 122
GOLDEN STATE TRANSPORTA-
    TION 122
Goodwill 17, 18, 21, 29, 113, 137
Grading of prospective names 129–
    132
Graphic design 101–106
GRASPEN 84, 85, 109

Greek language 3, 7, 58, 89, 94–98, 101
GREYHOUND **Preface**, 8, 32–37, 41, 75, 109, 122
Greyhound Corporation 32, 41
GREYHOUND SECURITIES 33
GWRI 79

H

HALLMARK 41, 126
Handle 13, **Glossary**
HANG TEN 16, 37, 51, 68, 76, 80, 109, 126
Hang Ten International 16
HEALTH CARE CHOICE **Preface**, 112
Heileman Brewing Co. 25
Henri's Food Products Company, Inc. 86
HENRI'S TAS-TEE DRESSING 87
HERE'S JOHNNY 81
Here's Johnny Portable Toilet, Inc. 81
HERE'S JOHNNY RESTAURANTS 81
Hermetic names 96
HIB-IMMUNE 125
HIBVAX 125
HOLIDAY ON ICE 88
HOLSUM 86
Homonyms 30, **Glossary**
Humor 80, 89, 109
HYBRINETICS 96
Hyphenation 84

I

IBM 44, 103
ICE CAPADE 88
Ideophones, ideophonemes, 90, 91, **Glossary**

Idiot Searches, 115, 118, **Glossary**
IMPALA 5, 75
IMPERIAL 71
Impression 5, 59, 74, 84, 88
Incontestability 117
Indo-European language 94
INDUCTOSYN 96
INDUSTRIAL NATIONAL CORPO-RATION 18
Information 68, 69
Infringement 29, 43, 112–116
Initials 30, 32
Injunction 29, 34, 43, **Glossary**
INTEGRA 60, 61, 100
Intellectual property 15, 114, **Glossary**
Internal Revenue Service 21
INTERNATIONAL BUSINESS MA-CHINES 44
Interrogatories 42, **Glossary**
Involvement of customer *see* Personal involvement
Italian language 95
IVORY 8

J

JAG 86
JAGUAR 75, 86, 109
Japanese language 30
JELLIBEANS 34–37, 40–42, 44, 51, 59, 78, 79, 109, 115, 122, 125
JELL-O 86
Jingle 53, 54, 68, **Glossary**
JOGSTRAP 80
JOHN HANCOCK MUTUAL LIFE INSURANCE CO. 77
Johnny Carson Apparel 81
JOLLY GREEN GIANT 107, 109
JONES 20
JOVAN 91
JOYA 91

K

KAL-DEK 36
KANON 87
KELVINATOR 95
Kerosene 137
KITCHENAID 83
King's English 57–60, 102
KLEENEX 36, 100
KODAK **Preface**, 14, 23, 36–41, 44,
    109, 126
KOMPACK 36
KOOL-AID 84
Korean Language, 30
KOTEX 36

L

Lanham Act 21, 111, 112, 117, 118,
    135, **Glossary**
Latches 137
Latin Language 58–60, 86, 88, 89,
    93–97
LAUNDROMAT 88
Legal clout *see* Legal strength
Legal considerations 11, 39–45, 49
Legal strength 12, 36, 37, 39–45,
    99, 103, 113, 115, 118, 119,
    123–126
LEGG'S 80
License 15, 16, 137, **Glossary**
Life of product 62
LIGHT 25
Likelihood of confusion 28, 81, 87,
    103, 115, 121, 124, 135, 137
LILAC LADY 75
LILY PADS 75
Linguistics 5
LING TEMKO VOUGHT 29
Linoleum 137, 138
LITE 11, 24, 39, 44, 69
Logos 103–106, 133

LOLLIPOPS 34, 41, 115, 122, 125
Loss of ownership 136–138
LOVE'S 87
LTV 29
LUCITE 9, 89, 109

M

3M 30
MACINTOSH 99
MACHO 69
MANPOWER 109
MARATHON 77
Market considerations 11–13
Marketing factors 126–132
Marketing personel **Preface**, 49,
    52–54, 69, 70
Markings 138, 139
MAXIMA 100
MAXIMAGE 84
Meaning 5, 59, 78, 84, 88
Merchandizing 15, 17, 118,
    Glossary
Merely descriptive names 87, 103,
    122, 124
MERIT 58
METHOCARBAMOL 58
Metonymy 76, 109, **Glossary**
Metro Goldwyn Mayer 75
Mexican language 64
MICRA 100
MICROKERATOME 98
MICROLAND 27
MICRO-LOK 36
MICROPHASE 85
Miller Brewing Company, Inc. 24, 69
Mimicking monikers 86, 87
MINNESOTA MINING AND MAN-
    UFACTURING, Co. 29
MINUTEMAID 88, 100
Misuse of a name 136, 137
MIURA 75

MOMAR 91
MONAVE 91
MONITORQUE 84
MOONDANCE 84
Morphemes 88, **Glossary**
Motion to strike 42, **Glossary**
MR BUBBLE 59
MR CLEAN 59, 107
MR GOODWRENCH 5, 97
MR MAGOO 107
Multimedia names 91, 92
MUMPSVAX 79
MUSTANG 99
MYRDDIN 79

N

Naked license 137
NATIONAL CASH REGISTER 29
N.B.I. **Preface**
NCR 29
NEO-SYNEPHRIN 98
NIGHT FUCHSIA 75
Norman language 94
Notices 138
NOVA 30, 79
NUMBERJACK 88
Nylon 137
NYQUIL 35, 38, 98

O

Obscene names 30, 31, 60
Ogilvy, David **Preface**, 70
OILEX 40
Oklahoma Osteopathic Hospital
    Preface, 54, 112
OLD HEARTH 40
OMNIFAX 95
Onomatopes 78, 82, 89, 99, 109,
    Glossary

Onamatopoeia, Onomatopoeic, *see*
    Onomatopes
Opposition to registration 116, 141
Originality 99, 100, 124
Orthography 83, **Glossary**
Owens Corning 107
Ownership 134–137
OZARK 99

P

PALMOLIVE 84
PAN AM 86
PAN AMERICAN 85, 95
PAPERMATE 59, 100
Paris Convention 117, 118
PARROT JUNGLE 40
Patents 14, 15
Patent Office *see* U.S. Patent &
    Trademark Office
Patronyms 20–22, **Glossary**
PEDALINA 91
Pei, Mario 10, 97, **Bibliography**
PENCIL 24
Pemberton, John Styth 25,79
Penetration 108–110, 129, 131
PEPSI COLA 78
PEPSI LIGHT 25
PERFORMULA 85
PERRIER 30
Personal involvement 68, 69, 109,
    127–132
PET ROCK 62
Phonestheme, 91
Phonetic impact *see* Aural impact
Phonological syntagmeme 91
Phonosememe 91
PIED PIPER 109
PILLARS SECURITIES 130, 131
Pillsbury Company 107
PINK PANTHER 107

PINTO 17
PLAYBOY 17
PLAYSKOOL 97
PLUG-O-MATIC 84
Poetry 78–80, 109
POLYMERIN 95
PONY 125
Pope, Alexander 6, 143
POPPIN'FRESH 107
Portemanteau words 88
Positioning 13–15, 27
POWERBUILT 58
POZ-I-LOK 36
Preliminary injunction 43, 116
PREST-O-LITE 87
Principal Register 118
Priority 27, 110, 117, 140
Procter & Gamble 8
Procter, Harley 8
Product life 62
Profit 15–19
PROMO 58
Promotion 12
PRO-SLIDE 85
PRO-TEK 85
Proto-Indo-European language 94
Provencal language 94–96,
    Glossary
PSCHITT 31
Psychology 10, 49, 129
PUMPHOUSE 77, 91, 109
Pumphouse Gang (The) 91
PYREX 100

Recapitulation 107–110
Reference *see* Evocative reference
REGAINE 86
Registrability 116–118
Registration 22, 112, 116, 135, 139–
    141
®SYMBOL 139
REJUVIA 40
Request for admission 42
RE-SELL-IT 119
Restraining orders, 14, 42, 43, 116,
    Glossary
Retrogressive formation 86
Rhymes 79, 80, 109
Rhythm 78–80, 89, 109
RICE-KRISPIES 87
Richardson-Vicks 35
RIVIERA 58
Robert Keith & Co. 102
Robinson, Frank M. 25
ROCKY 99
Role model 76, 128
Romance languages 30, 60, 79, 95,
    97
ROMANCE STYLIST 13
ROSEBUDS 75
ROSEFAIR 75
RUBBERMAID 100
RUMPELSTILTSKIN 79

R

RAINBIRD **Preface**, 84, 97, 109
Rainier Brewing Co. 25
Rating system 121–132
RC COLA 25, 78
READER 11, 40

S

SAFARI 40
SAFARILAND 11
SANKA 138
SARA LEE **Preface**, 18
SCENFOLI 89, 101
Schlitz (Joseph) Brewing Co. 25
Scope of protection *see* Legal
    strength
SCRABBLE 89

SCORPION 75
Search *see* Availability search
Searching services 118, 119
Secondary meaning 44, 45,
    Glossary
SEIKO 87
Seizure of counterfeit goods 14, 29,
    42, 117
Semantation 88–90, 99, 109,
    Glossary
Semantemes 89
Semantics 10, 49, **Glossary**
Semants 89, 99, 128, **Glossary**
Semonemics 3, **Glossary**
Semonemic techniques 107–110
SENTRA 100
SERGIO VALENTE 17
Service mark 5, 16, 111, 124, 135,
    Glossary
Sesquipedalianism 96
SEVEN SEAS LODGE 77
SEYCOS 87
Shakespeare, William 9
SHASTA 10, 13, 76
SHY VIOLET 75
SIDEKICK 80
SILK 8
SILKEASE 91
Similarity 124–126, 131
SINFOLY 101
SKYHAWK 75
SLICKCRAFT 40
SLIME 9
SMITH 20
SOCIAL SECURITY 80
Sociology 10
Sonority 80
Spanish language 32, 60, 64, 79, 95
Spelling 87, 101
SPIDER 75
STAINMASTER 100
Standard Oil of New Jersey 117

STANZA 100
STARION 9
STRATEGO 86, 109
Strength of a name *see* Legal
    Strength
STRIDE 58
SUBURBANK 85, 129–132
SUDAFED 98
Suggestive name 33, 39, 40, 44, 124
Summary judgment 43, **Glossary**
Summary proceedings 15, 42, 43
SUNBIRD 75
SUNBURST BANK 130
SUN-DROP 84
SUNKIST Preface, 84, 97
SUPER GLUE 11, 44
Supplemental Register 118
SUPRA 100
SURE 115
SURE & NATURAL 115
SURGICENTERS 40
Surnames *see* Patronyms
Surveys 127
Swinburne, Charles **Preface**
Symbolism 74–76, 81, 84, 89, 99,
    109
Symmetry 36, 79, 109
Sympiptism 7, 89, 109, **Glossary**
SYMPHOLY 101
Synthesis 50–51, 70–73
SYNTRON 95

T

TAB 25
Tacking 85, 86, 109, **Glossary**
TARGET 98, 125
TAS-TEE 87
TASTY 87
Tasty Snacks, Inc. 87
TAURUS 75

Taxation 18, 21
TAYLOR 21
Technicians' names 5, 26
TEENPLAN 130
TEFLON **Preface**
TELEDYNE 95
TELEMART 95
TELEMED 40
Television commercial 67–72
TELOPHASE 96
TEMPLAR BANK 129–132
TENDER VITTLES 29
Thermos 137
THISTLE 59
THUNDERBIRD 75
TIGER 7, 91
TKO 91
TOLFAN **Preface**
TOPBRASS 127–128
TOUCH-O-MATIC 84
Toyota 61
Trademark Attorneys 28, 114, 119
Trademark Counterfeiting Act 117
Trademarks 5, 15, 111, 135,
    Glossary
Trademark Trial and Appeal Board
    140
Trade names 5, 111, 124, 134,
    Glossary
TRAILWAYS 34
TRANSAMERICA 95
TREDIA 100
TWINKIES 59
Typesetting 102
Typography 102

U

UAL, Inc. 60
ULTRASUEDE 40
UN-COLA (The) 26

UNDERNEATH IT ALL 40
Unfair competition 11
United Airlines 60
United Distributors, Inc. 105
Upjohn Co. 86
U.S. Congress 111, 141
U.S. Customs Service 14, 116
Use in commerce 134–136
U.S. Education Department 59
U.S. Patent & Trademark Office
    Preface, 9, 98, 103, 111, 115,
    116, 139, 140

V

VELCRO 14
VETTE 86
VICKS VAPORUB 35
VISA 40
VISION CENTER 40
VITA-LIFE 84
VITALIS 95
Vocable 6, 122, **Glossary**
Vocabulary 51, 58–61

W

WALKMAN 99
WATCHMAN 99
WATERPIK 83
William the Conqueror 75
WINDBLOSSOMS 84
WINDSURFER 11
WINE CHILLER 26
WINE COOLER 26
Wolf, Tom 91
WORKMATE 100
WUV'S 87

X, Y, Z

XEROX 91, 138
XEROX CORPORATION 18
XYTRONYX 96
YVES SAINT LAURENT 17, 22

YOLAI 91
YU 91
ZIPPER 109
ZZOTTI 91